Seven Keys to Hearing God's Voice

Endorsements

In *Seven Keys to Hearing God's Voice,* Craig von Buseck does a masterful job of coaching believers on their journey to fulfill their prophetic destinies in Christ. This path of destiny is often complicated by the various decisions and choices one must make as well as in determining the specific will of God, which at times may seem to defy human reasoning. This book will release faith to hear God's Voice and to embrace the full counsel of God, empowering each one to find God's unique path for their lives.

TOM AND JANE HAMON, D.MIN/D. MIN
APOSTLES, VISION CHURCH @ CHRISTIAN INTERNATIONAL

Every believer wants to hear the voice of the Holy Spirit. In *Seven Keys to Hearing God's Voice,* Craig von Buseck gives us the "keys" to do just that and more...

WENDY GRIFFITH
700 CLUB CO-HOST
AUTHOR OF *YOU ARE A PRIZE TO BE WON*
CO-AUTHOR OF *PRAYING THE NEWS*

Craig has always been a forward-thinking communicator and leader, and this impactful book is no different. Not only did I admire it...I NEEDED it. Trust me, you do, too.

DALLAS JENKINS
DIRECTOR, "THE CHOSEN,"
"THE RESURRECTION OF GAVIN STONE"

God loves to communicate. He constantly speaks to us through many ways. He speaks through His anointed and powerful Word, the Bible. He speaks to us through the prodding of the Holy Spirit. He also speaks to us in a soft and gentle voice whenever we pray. Craig von Buseck's *Seven Keys to Hearing God's Voice* takes us on an exciting journey to discover and hear, and identify and sharpen our spiritual senses in knowing God's voice. Life is filled with many "crossroad moments" and we need to be sure we take the right path. This book will help you know how to discern His voice. Listen closely to what God is saying to know His plan for your life.

PETER M. KAIRUZ
PRESIDENT AND CEO, CBN ASIA, INC.
HOST OF THE 700 CLUB ASIA

I'd always heard I should pray to get God's guidance, but so many times I wanted to understand how that worked in more practical terms. Dr. Craig von Buseck has opened the gates of understanding for me with his book, *Seven Keys to Hearing God's Voice*. I've found both practical and biblical application that are encouraging, educational, and excellent! If you've wondered how to figure out God's will in your life, you'll love this book! You'll say, "I get it now!" just like me.

ANGELA BREIDENBACH
PRESIDENT, CHRISTIAN AUTHORS NETWORK
AUTHOR, SPEAKER, AND HOST OF LIT UP! RADIO

Honest, accurate, practical, and timely—a pastoral "must-read." Chapter Ten on acquiring confirmation from God struck me as being quite relevant for times as these—a world that has lost confidence in its God-counter-cultural worldviews and practices. Our God is a God of clear and concise confirmation for all who ask, knock, and seek.

TONY J. MARINO, MBA
CO-FOUNDER AND HOST, *ALIVE IN CHRIST* RADIO

I have taught principles of how to recognize the voice and intentions of God for our lives for the last 30 years here in the U.S. as well as abroad. Craig has done a masterful job as he has taken the most comprehensive approach to date in order to accurately discern what is divinely inspired versus soul-influenced. I highly recommend this book for serious seekers of wisdom for themselves.

REV. TRAVIS THIGPEN
GATEWAY PROPHETIC TRAINING, RICHMOND, VA

Seven Keys To Hearing God's Voice is well-written godly counsel. The Scripture is central and the book is wise and God-honoring. The section on the proper place of personal prophecy is the best that I have read. It is also a delightful read, and the wonderful illustrations are apt and to the point. I heartily recommend Craig von Buseck's book to any Christian who wishes to know God's will for their life and ministry.

JOHN EDMISTON
FOUNDER AND CEO, *CYBERMISSIONS.ORG*

In a fever of information, alternatives and options, to hear His voice and to understand His will for any decision or project is crucial. In this season there are new things which we experience, there are places we have never been through, there are stages which we cannot overcome so we must follow a direct divine guidance.

The book of Craig von Buseck is a guide, a challenge for each leader from modern Christian media.

TUDOR PETAN
PRESIDENT, *ALFA OMEGA TV MEDIA MINISTRY*, ROMANIA

Have you ever struggled with understanding God's will for your life? I know I have had my seasons of searching. In nearly fifty years of being a Christ follower, I have learned that the Lord speaks to us on multiple levels, and some of these are not discussed in some of our churches.

That is why I am excited to proudly endorse Craig von Buseck's new book *Seven Keys to Hearing God's Voice*. Craig provides a fresh, contemporary look the various ways that God reveals and authenticates his will to believing people. His unique perspective as a minister, chaplain, and communicator guide the reader through an invigorating and revitalizing journey through Scripture to discover the many ways that God has and continues to speak to His people.

I know that you will be blessed as you read this insightful book.

JOHN H. THURMAN JR., M.DIV., M.A.
THERAPIST, SPEAKER,
#1 AMAZON BEST SELLING AUTHOR

Craig von Buseck's book is a very detailed and thought-provoking read. It challenges the reader to go deeper in their personal relationship with the Lord. People need to know that God is still the same omniscient God and He is still speaking to us today ... and yes, His sheep shall know His voice. Craig's detailed outline gives great revelation of how to "Get a hold of God!" and how to discern His voice. I love that it's all based on Scripture. This is a must read for anyone who is longing to hear God's voice and grow deeper and stronger in a relationship with Him.

NINA KEEGAN
GRACE GRACE WITH NINA KEEGAN AND MICHELLE HUMPHREYS

One night as I sat in a smoky bar in London, a spiritual renewal began in my life that set me on a search for truth. I had grown up the son of missionary parents and had once worked for Billy Graham, but at that point in my career I was a tabloid journalist caught up in that hard-working, hard-drinking world. On that night, I finally awoke to the leading of the Holy Spirit at work in my life. That was the first step to a ministry that has taken me around the world, interviewing Christian leaders and the heroes of the suffering church. In his book, *Seven Keys to Hearing God's Voice*, Craig von Buseck provides both a biblical and practical guide to the way God guides believers who are humbly seeking Him for direction. Just as I was led by the Holy Spirit into this amazing adventure as a Christian journalist, you too can discover God's call on your life, learning to hear His voice and follow His guidance.

DAN WOODING
FOUNDER, *ASSIST* NEWS SERVICE
HOST, *FRONT PAGE RADIO*

If you have questions about finding God's will for your life, I'm confident you'll find the answers in Craig von Buseck's outstanding book, *Seven Keys to Hearing God's Voice*. God's will is the only place you can experience deep and lasting peace—and every other spiritual blessing as well. With the help of this book's insights, your spiritual vision will become clearer, and you'll be drawn ever closer to very heart of God. Get ready for a life-changing encounter with the lover of your soul!

JIM BUCHAN
DIRECTOR OF PARTNER COMMUNICATIONS,
INSPIRATION MINISTRIES
FORMER MANAGING EDITOR OF
MINISTRY MAGAZINE AND THE *MORNINGSTAR JOURNAL*

A much-needed book for believers! At a time when many are seeking answers and direction, Craig delivers fail-proof and practical guidance on how to hear the voice of God.

CHARLENE AARON
CBN NEWS ANCHOR AND REPORTER

I've had the privilege of ministering with Craig von Buseck in the past, and what I respect about him is transferred throughout this timely, user-friendly guide on hearing God's voice. He presents a balance of theological insight, relatable teaching, and prophetic provocation. If you are on the fence about whether or not God still speaks today, this book provides a Bible-based theology for a speaking God. But don't expect anything stuffy. Craig's writing is engaging and relational. Also prepare to be provoked to experience the prophetic voice of the Spirit in new ways that were perhaps off your grid.

Perhaps the essence of the book is summed up best in the following statement: *"In order to combat the forces of darkness, Christians must learn to hear the voice of God in this generation so they can obey God's leading in their lives. This is a critical time in history. On all levels, God's people need to be in tune with what the Spirit of God is saying."*

Seven Keys to Hearing God's Voice will supernaturally activate you to begin hearing God speak with greater clarity and discernment! This book doesn't just tell you what to do; it shows you how to do it!

LARRY SPARKS, MDIV., REGENT UNIVERSITY
PUBLISHER, DESTINY IMAGE
AUTHOR OF *BREAKTHROUGH FAITH*
CO-AUTHOR OF *THE FIRE THAT NEVER SLEEPS* WITH
DR. MICHAEL BROWN AND JOHN KILPATRICK

Oh how I appreciate Craig von Buseck's heart in *Seven Keys to Hearing God's Voice.* There's such blessing in thinking harder and deeper about the will of God. When it comes to deep thinking, okay let's be real, that's probably not my best thing. But for this? I'm in. I'm in deeply.

RHONDA RHEA
TV PERSONALITY, AWARD-WINNING HUMOR COLUMNIST
AUTHOR OF 14 BOOKS, INCLUDING *MESSY TO MEANINGFUL,*
TURTLES IN THE ROAD, AND FIX *HER UPPER*

Seven Keys to Hearing God's Voice

By Dr. Craig von Buseck

RAMCASTLE PRESS

Copyright © 2018 by
Craig von Buseck

All rights reserved. No part of this book shall be reproduced or transmitted in any form or by any means, electronic, mechanical, magnetic, photographic including photocopying, recording or by any information storage and retrieval system, without prior written permission of the publisher. No patent liability is assumed with respect to the use of the information contained herein. Although every precaution has been taken in the preparation of this book, the publisher and author assume no responsibility for errors or omissions. Neither is any liability assumed for damages resulting from the use of the information contained herein.

Ramcastle Press

ISBN 978-1-7324991-0-2 (print book)
ISBN 978-1-7324991-1-9 (e-book)
Visit Author at **www.vonbuseck.com**
book and e-book designed and formatted by
ebooklistingservices.com

Scripture quotations marked **AMPC** are taken from the Amplified® Bible (AMPC). Copyright © 1954, 1958, 1962, 1964, 1965, 1987, 2015 by The Lockman Foundation. Used by permission.

Scripture quotations marked **ESV** are from the ESV® Bible (The Holy Bible, English Standard Version®), copyright © 2001 by Crossway, a publishing ministry of Good News Publishers. Used by permission. All rights reserved.

Scripture quotations marked **KJV** are taken from The Holy Bible, King James Version, 1611. Public Domain.

Scripture quotations marked **NASB** taken from the New American Standard Bible® (NASB). Copyright © 1960, 1962, 1963, 1968, 1971, 1972, 1973, 1975, 1977, 1995 by The Lockman Foundation. Used by permission.

Scripture quotations marked **NIV** are taken from the Holy Bible, New International Version®, NIV®. Copyright © 1973, 1978, 1984, 2011 by Biblica, Inc.™ Used by permission of Zondervan. All rights reserved worldwide. www.zondervan.com The "NIV" and "New International Version" are trademarks registered in the United States Patent and Trademark Office by Biblica, Inc.™

Scripture quotations marked **NKJV** are taken from the New King James Version®. Copyright © 1982 by Thomas Nelson. Used by permission. All rights reserved.

Scripture quotations marked **NLT** are taken from the Holy Bible, New Living Translation, copyright ©1996, 2004, 2015 by Tyndale House Foundation. Used by permission of Tyndale House Publishers, Inc., Carol Stream, Illinois 60188. All rights reserved.

Library of Congress Cataloguing-in-Publishing Data

Von Buseck, Craig Charles.

    Seven keys to hearing God's voice / by Dr. Craig von Buseck.

    Includes bibliographical references. | Lancaster, SC: Ramcastle Press, 2018.

    978-1-7324991-0-2 (pbk.) | 978-1-7324991-1-9 (ebook) |

LCCN 2018951737

1. Listening--Religious aspects--Christianity. 2. God (Christianity)--Knowableness. |
BISAC RELIGION / Christian Life / Spiritual Growth
BV4509.5 V66 2018 | DDC 231/.042--dc23

1 3 5 7 9 10 8 6 4 2
Printed in the United States of America

Dedication

To my dear mother, Carol von Buseck. You have always been an enduring support to your children and grandchildren as we pursued God's plan for our lives. Your steadfast faith and devotion to God and His principles has been a rock upon which our family life was established. Thank you for the love you have shown to all of us.

Table of Contents

FOREWORD
    By Isik Abla..xvii
INTRODUCTION
    Guidance Comes from Having a Relationship......................1
CHAPTER ONE
    God is Love—and Love Communicates...............................7
CHAPTER TWO
    What are the Seven Keys to God's Guidance?.....................31
CHAPTER THREE
    Tuning in to God's Frequency..49
CHAPTER FOUR
    The Scriptures—God Speaks Through His Inspired Word.......65
CHAPTER FIVE
    The Leading of the Holy Spirit—Learning to Recognize
    God's Still, Small Voice...87
CHAPTER SIX
    Hearing God's Voice Through Desires, Dreams
    & Visions...109
CHAPTER SEVEN
    Godly Counsel—the Wisdom and Experience of Others......129
CHAPTER EIGHT
    Peace—Reaping the Fruit of Hearing God's Voice............147
CHAPTER NINE
    Personal Prophecy—Hearing God's Specific Voice to You...161
CHAPTER TEN
    Confirmation—Hearing God Again, and Again, and Again...185
CHAPTER ELEVEN
    Circumstances—Hearing God in Every Day Life............205
CHAPTER TWELVE
    Truly Hearing God—Seeking the Maker of the Stars.......227
Bibliography..249

About the Author..253

Foreword

As a new Muslim covert, when I first came to Christ I was not familiar with the voice of God. The church I attended didn't teach about hearing from God. The Holy Spirit wasn't emphasized. Then to my surprise, I started hearing God's inner voice. I was hearing His gentle whisper and it was very sweet. But I didn't know how to continue my relationship with Him.

I didn't know how to grow without any teaching or discipleship tool that would help me. I felt lost.

Then I started attending a new church that taught from the Word of God about the Holy Spirit as a Person of the Trinity. I started highlighting in my Bible that He is the Spirit of truth. He is the Comforter. He is the Counselor. The Holy Spirit will tell you, Jesus said, what you need to say.

I started reading and praying the Word of God, and inviting the Holy Spirit to come, in Jesus' name.

I didn't know how to seek and find the guidance of God and know His will for my life. But I learned through various Bible teachers and by reading God's Word. This helped me and I started hearing His voice in my inner being. But I had no idea how to go deeper with Him through the leading of the Holy Spirit.

In time I have learned to pay attention to that small whisper and obey it.

I wish I had read Craig's book, *Seven Keys to Hearing God's Voice* at the very beginning of my walk. It would have given me the help I needed at that time. I needed to learn how recognize God's voice, and how to separate it from the other voices we hear. It took me many years to learn the truths that Craig teaches in this powerful work.

Many times we wonder about God's will for us and feel lost in our walk with Christ. Hearing God's voice and obeying that voice are two different things. A lot of believers have a hard time hearing the voice of God – and many have difficulty obeying His voice. Discernment is lacking in the Body of Christ and we are living times where it is most needed and important. *Seven Keys to Hearing God's Voice* provides clear help and guidance to every believer to distinguish God's will from their own.

This book teaches the short cuts—I would call these the answers I was seeking for so many years. It teaches the basic principles of abiding in Him; knowing how to hear God's voice; and learning how to seek His will and guidance. Dr. Craig von Buseck explains that when we pray and abide in Jesus we will start to hear from Him more clearly and He will direct our path in the best way.

Seven Keys to Hearing God's Voice teaches us how to put the Word of God into practice. The guidance this book provides will make a life-long impact in every believer's life.

Isik Abla

Founder & President of *Isik Abla Ministries TV*
Social Media Evangelist to the Muslim World

Seven Keys to Hearing God's Voice

Introduction

Guidance Comes from Having a Relationship

*T*he Chinese have a symbol in their language to represent the concept of happiness—it's a man and a woman walking in a garden with God. I believe this image has been passed down through generations of Chinese, most likely originating with our ancestors, Adam and Eve. Life, as God originally designed it in the Garden of Eden, was absolute bliss as mankind communed with God.

This is still the source of joy and peace—and it is what God intended from the beginning.

The writer of Genesis tells us that God walked with Adam and Eve in the cool of the day (Genesis 3:8). They interacted face-to-face. Sin had not yet entered the world, so there was nothing separating God and man.

Imagine how glorious that must have been.

Adam and Eve never wondered if God loved them. He demonstrated that love on a daily basis. There was no questioning of God's will. He communicated His desires to them face to face. There were no feelings of rejection, misunderstanding, bewilderment, or confusion. There was just perfect love, acceptance, and clarity of vision.

Why? Because God communicated with them every day and they heard His voice.

"Good for them," you may be saying. And like the matchmaker, Yenta in *Fiddler on the Roof*, you may add, "But this place is no Garden of Eden." [1]

You're right. Adam and Eve disobeyed God's command concerning eating from the tree of the knowledge of good and evil, and they gave their allegiance over to the serpent, Lucifer, the enemy of God. When they did that, sin entered this world. From that moment forward, sinful man was separated from a holy God and our communication with Him was hindered.

But God always wanted a family. That's why He created mankind in the first place. Because God is love, He yearned to once again live in relationship with us. It was never God's intention that there be separation between Himself and His creation.

And so He set in motion a plan to bridge the divide caused by sin by sending His Son, Jesus, to save mankind and restore fellowship with Him. By dying on the cross, Jesus

---

[1] Stein, Joseph. *Fiddler on the Roof*, 1971, Metro-Goldwyn-Mayer Studios.

paid the price for the sin that separated us from Him, so now we can have daily relationship with God. Then Jesus sent the Holy Spirit to live within us, enabling us to once again hear His voice and walk in relationship day-to-day.

Learning how to hear God and be led through this relationship with the Holy Spirit is what this book is all about!

Years ago when I was in college, I did an internship at a local public broadcasting station. I worked in the production department creating commercials for corporate sponsors. One day the donor representative was along for the ride to a video shoot. This young lady told us she was thinking about purchasing a duplex, but she wasn't sure if she was making a wise move. She made a comment I will never forget. "There are so many roads I could follow. How do you know you're making the right decisions in life?"

That's the question of the ages, isn't it?

The great news is that as Christians, we can learn to discern God's will in major decisions. God wants to communicate with us and share His will for our lives.

He is talking—are you listening?

God Wants to Lead His Children

Every person has at one time wondered if they are making the right choices in life. For the person who doesn't know God, it may merely be a question of survival and self-promotion. But for the believer, it is the cry of the heart to do what is pleasing for our Heavenly Father.

God created us to have intimate fellowship with Him. He wants to reveal Himself to us, and to communicate with us. But it's not always easy for us to know that we are actually hearing His voice. When the Holocaust survivor, Corrie Ten Boom, was in a Nazi concentration camp, she experienced doubt about God's willingness to direct her steps:

> I remember that once when I looked on the stars I said, "O Lord, all the stars are in Your guidance, but have You forgotten Your child?" I had my Bible with me and that was such a great joy. In the Bible I read that the hairs of our head are numbered, and God has all the universe in His hands. That means that God has a telescope and a microscope.[2]

In His awesome power, God uses His telescope to rule the universe. But in His love and compassion, He also has His microscope focused on your concerns and the decisions you are facing. We serve Almighty God, who is also our loving Heavenly Daddy.

The Bible tells us that we are to seek to become like Jesus—growing

> ...to the measure of the stature of the fullness of Christ.
> —Ephesians 4:13b, NKJV

Jesus set the example for those who want to know God and do His will when He declared,

> ...I will do what the Father requires of me, so that the world will know that I love the Father.
> —John 14:31, NLT

---

[2] Ten Boom, Corrie, "A Faith Not Hidden," interview with Pat Robertson, The 700 Club, Christian Broadcasting Network, 1974.

Even in His darkest hour, as He faced the horror of crucifixion in the Garden of Gethsemane, Jesus prayed,

> He went on a little farther and bowed with his face to the ground, praying, "My Father! If it is possible, let this cup of suffering be taken away from me. Yet I want your will to be done, not mine."
> —Matthew 26:39, NLT

In order to grow into maturity as a Christian and learn how to hear the voice of God, we must follow this example from one of the most difficult moments in the life of Jesus.

We must have the same humility as John the Baptist who declared of Jesus, *"He must increase, but I must decrease."* When we make the humble pursuit of God's will our goal, we discover that our spiritual sensitivity will grow by leaps and bounds—and this is God's promise to us. As the psalmist declares,

> The Lord directs the steps of the godly. He delights in every detail of their lives.
> —Psalms 37:23, NLT

In other words, God is delighted when we desire for Him to order our steps!

We were created with the ability to hear God speaking to us—we just need to learn how to tune into His frequency. That is what this book is all about. Do you want to know how to hear God's voice and follow His guidance for your life? Then read on!

Chapter One

God is Love – and Love Communicates

ne thing we can see clearly throughout the Bible is that God communicates with His people. He does it in many different ways, but the undeniable fact is that God speaks to us. Because God is love, He desires communication with His children. He created mankind in order to have a relationship with us. It was never God's intention for any separation to exist between Himself and His creation. The God of the Bible is a personal God who desires intimate fellowship. King David declared the wonderful love of our heavenly Father toward each living human being:

> How precious also are Your thoughts about me, O God! They cannot be numbered! I can't even count them; they

outnumber the grains of sand! And when I wake up, you are still with me!

—Psalms 139:17-18, NLT

Yet because God is love, He also created man with the freedom of choice. God didn't create a race of robots—he created mankind in His image, with the ability to think, to feel, to love, and to feel the pain of rejection. Only a loving God would give man the freedom to choose not to obey Him. Without choice there is no love.

Despite man's fall into sin, there have always been people with a desire to know God and follow His ways. Throughout the Old Testament we see numerous examples of God communicating with individuals:

- God communicated with Adam and Eve.
  —Genesis 2:16-17; 3:9, 16-19

- God communicated with Cain.
  —Genesis 4:9-15

- God communicated with Enoch.
  —Genesis 5:24

- God communicated with Noah.
  —Genesis 6:13-21

- God communicated with Abraham.
  —Genesis 12:1-3; 15:1-21; 17:1-22; 22:1-2

- God communicated with Hagar.
  —Genesis 16:7-13

- God communicated with Abraham and Sarah.
  —Genesis 18:1-15

- God communicated with Rebekah.
  —Genesis 25:23

- God communicated with Isaac.
  —Genesis 26:2-5; 24

- God communicated with Jacob.
  —Genesis 28:13-15; 31:3

- God communicated with Pharaoh.
  —Genesis 41:28

- God communicated with Joseph.
  —Genesis 37:5-10

- God communicated with Moses.
  —Exodus 3:1-22; 4:1-17

- God communicated with Balaam, even through a donkey.
  —Numbers 22:12-35

- God communicated with Joshua.
  —Joshua 1:1-9; 5:13-15

- God communicated with Deborah.
  —Judges 4:6

- God communicated with Samuel.
  —1 Samuel 3:10-14

- God communicated with David.
  —1 Samuel 23:2

- God communicated with Solomon.
  —1 Kings 3:5-15

- God communicated with Job.

  —Job 38:1-41:34

- God communicated with Elijah.

  —1 Kings 19:11-18

- God communicated with Elisha.

  —2 Kings 6:8-12

- God communicated with Isaiah.

  —Isaiah 6:1-13

- God communicated with Jeremiah.

  —Jeremiah 1:4-10

In His love, God communicated with His people through the Old Testament prophets, declaring that He would send a Messiah, a Savior who would take away their sins, and restore communication between God and man. In this "New Covenant" God would not just speak through the prophets, but by His Holy Spirit, He would make Himself available to every person, one-to-one.

In his book, *Experiencing God*, Henry Blackaby writes:

> How God spoke in the Old Testament is not the most important factor. *That* He spoke is the crucial point.[3]

The prophet Jeremiah was given a glimpse of what this glorious new covenant would be like.

---

[3] Blackaby, Henry. "Experiencing God" Online: https://www.google.com/amp/s/todayswordfromgod.com/2015/11/09/god-speaks-part-1/amp

> "But this is the covenant which I will make with the house of Israel after those days," declares the Lord, "I will put My law within them and on their heart I will write it; and I will be their God, and they shall be My people. They will not teach again, each man his neighbor and each man his brother, saying, 'Know the Lord,' for they will all know Me, from the least of them to the greatest of them," declares the Lord, "for I will forgive their iniquity, and their sin I will remember no more."
> —Jeremiah 31:33-34, NASB

Jesus endured separation from His Father and the agony of the cross so we could once again enjoy God's presence and have the ability to hear His voice and communicate with Him.

At the point of Jesus' death, he cried out, "It is finished" (John 19:30). At that moment the veil in the temple that divided the people from the Holy of Holies was torn in half. There would be no more separation between God and man. Abba Father, our Daddy God, sent His Son to build a bridge across the chasm of sin so that we could walk with Him as Adam and Eve did in the cool of the day. Then Jesus sent the Holy Spirit to dwell with us on a permanent basis.

Jesus promised that we would literally hear His voice. Speaking of Himself as the Good Shepherd, He declared:

> ...the sheep follow him, for they know his voice. A stranger they will not follow, but they will flee from him, for they do not know the voice of strangers.
> —John 10:4b-5, ESV

As we saw in the Old Testament, there are also numerous examples in the New Testament of God communicating with individuals:

- God communicated with Joseph.
  —Matthew 1:20-23
- God communicated with the Wise Men.
  —Matthew 2:12
- God communicated with Zacharias.
  —Luke 1:11-20
- God communicated with Mary.
  —Luke 1:28-38
- God communicated with Simeon.
  —Luke 2:25-32
- God communicated with Pilate's wife.
  —Matthew 27 19
- God communicated with Philip.
  —Acts 8:26-40
- God communicated with Saul.
  —Acts 9:1-9
- God communicated with Ananias.
  —Acts 9:10-16
- God communicated with Cornelius.
  —Acts 10:1-7
- God communicated with Peter.
  —Acts 10:9-16
- God communicated with Paul.
  —Acts 16:6-10

- God communicated with Agabus.
  —Acts 11:27-30; 21:10-14
- God communicated with John.
  —Rev. 1:1-2, 10-20

Jesus rebuked the rebellious religious leaders of his day who were blind and deaf to God as a result of their sin and selfishness:

> He who belongs to God hears what God says. The reason you do not hear is that you do not belong to God.
> —John 8:47 NIV

If we belong to God, we will yearn to hear His voice. As we walk with Him and talk to Him, we can learn to discern what He says to us.

Now that you know the Bible promises you can hear His voice, you may wonder how God speaks to His people today.

The answer is, any way He wants to. He is God and He can choose any method to communicate with us. Many people have too small a view of God. They put Him in a box and say that He can only speak in one particular way—and typically it is the way with which they are most comfortable. But the truth is that God can do whatever He chooses. He is sovereign, and He can communicate in any way He desires.

But once again, because God is love, He has revealed in Scripture certain key ways in which He typically communicates with man. We can grow in confidence to know that God's speaking to man is just as normal as one person talking to another. That is the way He is. That is the way He has always been. That is the way He will always be.

What kind of a God would He be if He created us, but chose not to talk to us? Without the ability to communicate, there would be an eternal chasm between God and man. But through the sacrifice of Jesus, we can now spend daily time with God and learn how to hear His voice.

In Psalm 16:11, David demonstrated his confidence in God's guidance:

> You will show me the way of life granting me the joy of your presence and the pleasures of living with you forever.
> —Psalm 16:11, NLT

We Need to Hear God's Voice

We live in a fallen world that seems to be growing more dangerous every day. Events like the September 11th terrorist attacks, beheadings and torture by groups like ISIS and Al-Qaeda, and rogue nations threatening nuclear attack have jarred the world into a new reality. More Christians are being martyred around the world today than at any other time since the Roman era. Terror seems to be mounting on every side.

But as the darkness encroaches, the light of the Gospel shines ever brighter. With the explosion of communication through the Internet and digital media, there are also greater opportunities than ever before for preaching the Gospel of peace and love through Jesus Christ. As a result, more people are being won to Christ today than in the history of the world.

This is truly the finest hour of Christ's Church.

In order to combat the forces of darkness, Christians must learn to hear the voice of God in this generation so they can obey God's leading in their lives. This is a critical time in history. On all levels, God's people need to be in tune with what the Spirit of God is saying.

Parents need to listen for God's leading in raising their children. Pastors need to seek Divine guidance on how to shepherd their congregations. Government officials must humbly seek the Lord in setting policy for their nations. Business leaders need the spirit of Joseph and Daniel in creatively expanding their enterprises. Military planners must rely on the Spirit of the Lord to give them divine strategies for victory. Educators must seek the Lord for innovative ways to teach the skills needed for success in today's rapidly-changing world. Those in the entertainment world must be led by the Master Storyteller in creativity and excellence.

We live in a physical world that is controlled by certain natural laws—the law of gravity, the law of thermodynamics, and so on. But there is another realm that is just as real, though it is unseen—the world of the spirit. This unseen world is also controlled by certain spiritual laws, or principles, that are more powerful than most people can imagine. The authority to operate in this realm was opened to all Christians as a result of Jesus' death and resurrection, as He promised His disciples:

> All authority has been given to Me in heaven and on earth. Go therefore and make disciples of all nations...
> —Matthew 28:18b-19a NKJV

When Jesus sent out His disciples to begin the work of evangelism that we continue today, he gave them authority over Satan. Later Jesus extended that authority to the 70 when he sent them out to minister in His name.

> ...And heal the sick there, and say to them, "The kingdom of God has come near to you"... Then the seventy returned with joy, saying, "Lord, even the demons are subject to us in Your name." And He said to them, "I saw Satan fall like lightning from heaven. Behold, I give you the authority to trample on serpents and scorpions, and over all the power of the enemy, and nothing shall by any means hurt you."
>
> —Luke 10:9, 17-19 NKJV

This authority was extended to everyone who received Jesus as their Lord and Savior, thereby entering the Kingdom of God. As the Apostle Paul declared:

> And since we are his children, we are his heirs. In fact, together with Christ we are heirs of God's glory. But if we are to share his glory, we must also share his suffering.
>
> —Romans 8:17, NLT

That is why Jesus made what seems to be an audacious promise to his disciples when he said:

> I tell you the truth, anyone who believes in me will do the same works I have done, and even greater works, because I am going to be with the Father.
>
> —John 14:12, NLT

When Jesus went to the Father, He sent the Holy Spirit to dwell within us and to give us the power to do the things that Jesus did. Our job is to listen for the leading of the

Spirit, and then to step out in faith to do what He directs us to do.

This is all a part of working together with Jesus to build the Kingdom of God on earth.

Throughout His earthly ministry, Jesus spoke of this spiritual kingdom that has immense power over the natural world. It was not yet a physical place (though it will be in the fullness of time), but rather a spiritual realm where the people of God submit themselves to His will. In return, God provides them with spiritual power and authority—both in the physical world and in the world to come. Jesus declared:

> I tell you the truth, whatever you forbid on earth will be forbidden in heaven, and whatever you permit on earth will be permitted in heaven. I also tell you this: If two of you agree here on earth concerning anything you ask, my Father in heaven will do it for you.
> —Matthew 18:18-19, NLT

Seeing and Entering

Jesus gave insight into this unseen kingdom in a conversation with Nicodemus, a religious leader of the day:

> I tell you the truth, unless you are born again, you cannot *see the Kingdom of God*. ... I assure you, no one can *enter the Kingdom of God* without being born of water and the Spirit.
> —John 10:3 & 5, NLT, emphasis mine

Notice that the first time Jesus spoke of "seeing" the kingdom, and then later he referred to the experience of "entering" the kingdom. Our initial rebirth as Christians is like "seeing" the kingdom of God. But there is a deeper, richer experience of walking in the Spirit—and that comes when we "enter" the kingdom of God.

I compare "seeing" and "entering" the kingdom of God to the difference between the spectators in a stadium and the players on the field in a football game. The spectators are in the stands and they are watching the action. They identify with the team and they are excited about the game, but they are only "seeing" the contest, they aren't really participating. The players, on the other hand, are out on the field. They have "entered" the game and are working together to win. They have studied the playbook and even memorized the plays. They listen to the direction of the coach to receive the strategy to help them defeat their opponent. When they score, it is because they have worked together as a team under the leadership of the coach.

A person can be a believer and yet only "see" the things of the kingdom from the stands. But there is an amazing spiritual adventure available to the believer who "enters" the game—listening to the coach, working together as a team, studying the playbook and then walking in the manifestation of the Holy Spirit to score for the kingdom of God.

There is more to our Christian walk than just salvation and going to heaven—as wonderful as those things are. God has a plan, a personal destiny for each of us to fulfill. Through a personal relationship with Him, we can "enter" His Kingdom right here on Earth. The prayer of Jesus must also be our fervent desire:

May your Kingdom come soon. May your will be done on earth, as it is in heaven.
—Matthew 6:10, NLT

If we flip the word on its' head we have insight into its' meaning—"Kingdom" literally means "the **dom**inion of the **King**." In order for the Kingdom to be established in our lives, and in the Earth, we must learn to hear His voice so that we can then obey the will of the King.

That is the purpose of this book.

God's Plan for Your Life

In order to "enter" the Kingdom of God, you need to have a revelation that God loves you and He has an adventure prepared for you that is beyond your wildest dreams.

So why don't more people experience this amazing spiritual adventure?

In the last 100 years, many churches have downplayed, or even ignored, the truth that the Bible is the inerrant Word of God. People have been taught that they can pick and choose the parts of the Bible they want to embrace and the other parts they can ignore. Other so called Christian churches have taught that the Bible is merely a collection of moral stories and antiquated religious ideas—and that it is irrelevant for modern man.

Outside the church, the forces of Secular Humanism have invaded every center of power and influence in our culture in an attempt to drive biblical truth from the marketplace of ideas. There are generations today who are completely unaware of the truths of God and His universe.

For decades, public schools have been teaching our young people that they are accidental products of spontaneous evolution. To them, human beings are only one of the many evolving creatures on this planet—no more special than any other. There is nothing sacred about human life; there is no divine spark.

So, if everything is merely a result of some distant "big bang" then life is meaningless. If there is no God, there is no higher purpose in life. We should all just live for ourselves and get as much out of life as we can, because you only live once, and when you're dead, you're dead.

But for the person who is willing to think outside of this secular party line—to consider the clues that are shouting from the natural world, let alone the spiritual or metaphysical world, the universe displays overwhelming evidence of organization and intelligent design.

That's because a loving and intelligent God created it and sustains it. And the God who planned the universe has a wonderful plan for your life.

Did you know that you are the only person in the world who could be you? And those are staggering odds. According to Ali Binazir, a Harvard-educated medical doctor:

- The probability of your Dad meeting your Mom is 1 in 20,000.
- The probability of right sperm meeting right egg: 1 in 400 quadrillion.
- The probability of every one of your ancestors reproducing successfully is 1 in $10^{45,000}$

So the probability of your existing at all is 1 in $10^{2,685,000}$.[4]

Through a daily relationship with you, God wants to see you grow into a disciple who is unlike anyone else in the entire universe. God has a unique purpose for you to accomplish in life. There are things that God wants you to do that no one else can do. There are places that God wants you to go so that He can use you uniquely. And there are people that only you can reach.

When God made you He broke the mold—but He did not jettison the plan for your life. It's there waiting to be discovered. But you've got to go for it.

The things of God are free, but they're not cheap. He wants to give them to you, but He also wants you to show Him that you really want them. The only way to discover God's plan for your life is to learn how to hear His voice—and there's a price to be paid for that understanding.

"I buy that," you may be saying. "I want to live for God and do His will. That's why I'm reading this book. But I need some practical 'how-to's' to know if I'm actually hearing God's voice."

Fortunately, there is no formula that I can give you to help you to hear God.

"Fortunately?" you may respond. "Then why am I reading this book?"

---

[4] Binazir, Ali, http://blogs.harvard.edu/abinazir/2011/06/15/what-are-chances-you-would-be-born/)

I say *fortunately* because our walk with God is not a series of do's and don'ts, nor is it a recipe book that will give us the ingredients to produce the desired results. No, being a Christian and hearing His voice come by being in relationship with a personal God. Learning to hear His loving voice is a process of trial and error—just like learning to obey our earthly parents. And this is what makes the Christian walk of faith a most exciting adventure!

The Bible tells us that all things good come from God (James 1:17). Anything evil originates with Satan. So this is one of the first basic rules for learning how to discern God's voice from the Devil's. There are four voices that compete for our attention—God, the Devil, the world, and our own flesh. As we learn the principles of how to hear God's voice, and then apply them in a process of trial and error to the various messages that we are confronted with in life, we begin to have our senses exercised to discern between the voice of God, the voice of the evil one, the voice of the world, and the voice of our own carnal desires.

As you read through this book, I will be encouraging you to step out in faith to test your ability to discern between these four voices. I will audaciously dare to believe that you can hear God speaking to you. But the key word here is "believe." The writer of Hebrews declares:

> But without faith it is impossible to please Him, for he who comes to God must believe that He is, and that He is a rewarder of those who diligently seek Him.
>
> —Hebrews 11:6, NKJV

The key to unlocking the door to hearing from God is to take that step of faith. You can start by praying this simple prayer with me:

> Lord, I believe you have a plan for my life. I believe that if I seek your face and obey your commandments, you will reveal your will to me by your Spirit. So Father, I trust in your promise to guide my decisions. I believe you created me to hear your voice, and that you will lead me by your Holy Spirit. As your child, I want to know your plan for my life and to walk in your ways. I ask you to teach me to hear your voice as I seek you with all my heart. In Jesus' name, amen.

Seeking and Discerning God's Will

When you are diligent in your pursuit of God and in your desire to know His will, He will allow opportunities to come for you to learn how to discern His voice. These opportunities will require you to examine the various directions you could go. A business proposition or a potential relationship may come your way. These possible directions are either going to be in God's will for you, or they aren't. But because you desire to do God's will, when presented with these propositions, you will need to seek God's will through prayer.

When you cry out to Him saying, "Heavenly Father, make clear to me what your will is in this choice you have set before me," God will answer your prayer! But He will likely do so in a manner that will force you to engage in an analysis of what I call the seven keys of hearing God's voice:

- The Scriptures;
- The Holy Spirit speaking directly to your spirit;
- Godly counsel of mature Christian leaders;
- Peace or lack of peace in your spirit;
- Personal prophecy;
- Confirmation through multiple sources; and
- The circumstances surrounding the decision.

This book is an examination of these seven keys to help you learn how to begin the process of discerning God's voice from the other 3 voices: the evil one, the world, and our own carnal desires. As you step out in faith to hear God's voice, you may have an impression, or a peace deep inside you that a certain course of action is from God. You may receive advice from a pastor, friend, mentor, or a trusted family member that helps point you in a certain direction. Circumstances may arise that give you a clear indication that your choice is either a good or a bad one. The door may even close altogether. The business deal or relationship you are considering may simply fall through. But in this process of trial and error you are learning—and if you are diligent, in time you will begin to recognize God's voice and distinguish it from the others!

However the leading comes, you will need to take action on the basis of what you believe God is speaking to you through these seven keys. Once you have taken this step of faith, then you will need to wait to see what happens. It may turn out to be a wonderful decision, with an unmistakable outpouring of God's blessing. Or it could be that there is no immediate outward indication that is either positive or negative, and so you press on until time makes it clear that this choice was or was not of God. Then again, you may experience some negative consequences as a result of your choice, making it clear that you missed God's leading—and that's o.k. In all of this you're learning to hear and discern the voice of your Heavenly Father.

In every opportunity you will discover one of two things. You may come to realize that you made a mistake and the guidance wasn't really of God. In these cases, you must learn from your attempt at hearing God's voice and keep following the Lord the best you know how.

Or you may discover that the direction truly was from God. When this happens, there is an assurance that grows in your heart telling us that you really can hear God's voice— and you will take a giant step forward in your walk of faith. Instead of being like a little baby, crawling on the floor, by faith you have stood up in Christ and have taken your first teetering steps as a child of God. The more you do this, the stronger your steps become. Soon you find yourself walking, and then running in the exciting plans that God has for your life.

You may wonder if it is truly possible to hear God speaking to you. Rest assured, God created you with a measure of ability to hear His voice. That measure is multiplied when you accept Jesus Christ as your Lord and Savior, and then again when you are baptized in the Holy

Spirit. The question is will you use the gift that God has already placed within you?

A person just beginning to learn to hear the voice of God is like the boy Samuel. The Bible tells us that Samuel served in the temple under the High Priest, Eli. This was a time of corruption in Israel, and Scripture tells us that

> ...the word of the Lord was rare in those days; there was no frequent vision.
>
> —1 Samuel 3:1, ESV

Then Samuel's first lesson in hearing the voice of God began to unfold.

> Then the Lord called Samuel, and he said, "Here I am!" and ran to Eli and said, "Here I am, for you called me." But he said, "I did not call; lie down again." So he went and lay down.
>
> And the Lord called again, "Samuel!" and Samuel arose and went to Eli and said, "Here I am, for you called me." But he said, "I did not call, my son; lie down again." Now Samuel did not yet know the Lord, and the word of the Lord had not yet been revealed to him.
>
> And the Lord called Samuel again the third time. And he arose and went to Eli and said, "Here I am, for you called me." Then Eli perceived that the Lord was calling the boy. Therefore Eli said to Samuel, "Go, lie down, and if he calls you, you shall say, 'Speak, Lord, for your servant hears'"
>
> —1 Samuel 3:4-9, ESV

You see, Samuel could not yet discern between the voice of God and the voice of his master, Eli. In time, however, through his deep personal relationship with God, Samuel would grow to know His voice so well that he became one of the greatest prophets in the history of Israel.

Jesus promised that the New Testament believer would hear His voice. So like Samuel, you can also learn to hear the voice of God. Through the seven keys every possible leading can be weighed to tell whether it is a message from God, our flesh, the world, or from Satan. These keys are like a divine checklist when considering His guidance. By checking off the list, you can learn to discern God's voice in your life as well.

But in order to develop your ability to hear God's voice and receive His guidance you must maintain a daily relationship with Him. You have to surrender your life to God and submit every decision to His Lordship. When you do this, the Holy Spirit will guide you, instruct you, and even pour out His blessings on your life.

And when trials and tests come against you—because they come to all of us in this life—He will guide you through each one, and use the adversities in life to create His character in you. He promises to bring you through and into His best for your life.

> And we know that all things work together for good to those who love God, to those who are the called according to His purpose.
> —Romans 8:28 NKJV

My prayer is that this book will help you to better discern the voice of the Lord in your life, and through knowing His voice, you will grow to know and love Him more—because it's all about relationship.

Remember, the world needs what we've got.

"What do we have?" you may be asking.

As born again believers we are citizens of the Kingdom of God. We have Christ in us, the hope of glory! We have the Holy Spirit as our constant companion. Think of that. The world needs Jesus—Jesus lives in us—Jesus wants to use us to make Himself known to the world.

Jesus makes Himself real first to believers through these seven keys to God's guidance. Let's not just see the kingdom of God, but let's enter the Kingdom of God by daring to hear His voice and obey His call on our lives—because a life surrendered to God's plan is the greatest adventure imaginable!

Questions For Meditation

1. Do you believe that God wants to lead you into His will for your life? Why or why not?

2. How have you heard God's voice in the past?

3. How does God's love affect His desire to communicate with us?

4. Why do you think God hasn't provided a "formula" to be able to hear His voice and understand His will?

5. If God wants man to have authority in the earth, why are so few people experiencing it?

6. Describe God's method of communication in each of the following passages:

Then the angel said, "I am Gabriel! I stand in the very presence of God. It was he who sent me to bring you this good news!

—Luke 1:19, NLT

Some time later, the Lord spoke to Abram in a vision and said to him, "Do not be afraid, Abram, for I will protect you, and your reward will be great."

—Genesis 15:1, NLT

That night the Lord appeared to Solomon in a dream, and God said, "What do you want? Ask, and I will give it to you!"

—1 Kings 3:5, NLT

The Lord gave another message to Jeremiah. He said, "Go down to the potter's shop, and I will speak to you there." So I did as he told me and found the potter working at his wheel. But the jar he was making did not turn out as he had hoped, so he crushed it into a lump of clay again and started over.

Then the Lord gave me this message: "O Israel, can I not do to you as this potter has done to his clay? As the clay is in the potter's hand, so are you in my hand.

—Jeremiah 18:1-6, NLT

"Go out and stand before me on the mountain," the Lord told him. And as Elijah stood there, the Lord passed by, and a mighty windstorm hit the mountain. It was such a terrible blast that the rocks were torn loose, but the Lord was not in the wind. After the wind there was an earthquake, but the Lord was not in the earthquake. And after the earthquake there was a fire, but the Lord was not in the fire. And after the fire there was the sound of a gentle whisper. When Elijah heard it, he wrapped his face in his cloak and went out and stood at the entrance of the cave.

And a voice said, "What are you doing here, Elijah?'"

—1 Kings 19:11-13, NLT

Then the Lord told Moses, "Get up early in the morning and stand in Pharaoh's way as he goes down to the river. Say to him, 'This is what the Lord says: Let my people go, so they can worship me. If you refuse, then I will send swarms of flies on you, your officials, your people, and all the houses. The Egyptian homes will be filled with flies, and the ground will be covered with them. But this time I will spare the region of Goshen, where my people live. No flies will be found there. Then you will know that I am the Lord and that I am present even in the heart of your land. I will make a clear distinction between my people and your people. This miraculous sign will happen tomorrow."

And the Lord did just as he had said. A thick swarm of flies filled Pharaoh's palace and the houses of his officials. The whole land of Egypt was thrown into chaos by the flies.

Pharaoh called for Moses and Aaron. "All right! Go ahead and offer sacrifices to your God," he said. "But do it here in this land."

—Exodus 8:20-25, NLT

This is a revelation from Jesus Christ, which God gave him to show his servants the events that must soon take place. He sent an angel to present this revelation to his servant John, who faithfully reported everything he saw. This is his report of the word of God and the testimony of Jesus Christ...It was the Lord's Day, and I was worshiping in the Spirit. Suddenly, I heard behind me a loud voice like a trumpet blast.

—Revelation 1:1-2, 10, NLT

Chapter Two

What are the Seven Keys to God's Guidance?

I have no will but that of God.

—Brother Lawrence

When we were kids, one of my sister's favorite movies was *The Sound of Music*. In one key scene, the main character, a nun-in-training named Maria, has fled from her job as governess to the von Trapp family because she has fallen in love with their father, Captain von Trapp. When she seeks the counsel of the leader of the convent, the wise older woman asks, "What is the most important lesson you have learned here?"

Maria answers, "To find the will of God and to do it."

Good answer! This lesson led Maria to where she needed to be—back with the von Trapp family.

There are a myriad of questions we ask in life: "What am I going to do for a career? Where should I go to school? Should I take this job, or is there something better on the horizon? Whom should I marry?"

Life is a never-ending series of choices. How can we know whether we are making the right decisions? Do we rely on what the experts are saying or go with a gut feeling? Should we consult our horoscope? Maybe we should call the psychic hot line? Should we look to the stars—or should we seek the Maker of the stars?

As a disciple of Jesus Christ, you will eventually come to the realization that your life is not your own. In fact, that is what it means to make Jesus the Lord of your life. Your salvation depends on His Lordship. The apostle Paul, in the familiar passage, writes,

> If you openly declare that *Jesus is Lord* and believe in your heart that God raised him from the dead, *you will be saved*.
> —Romans 10:9, NLT, emphasis mine

Making Jesus the Lord of your life comes through having a personal relationship with Him, which helps you to understand who He wants you to be and what He wants you to do. This is a life-long process of discovery that only comes as a result of being sensitive to the leading of the Holy Spirit. Just like a trainer gently teaches a horse to respond to the bit, bridle, and harness, the Lord's work in our lives is meant to wean us from seeking our own will and teach us how to follow His leading.

For several years I served as the Spiritual Life producer at CBN.com, the online magazine of the Christian Broadcasting Network. I received this e-mail in response to my article "The Harness of the Holy Spirit":

> Your article is typical of many books I have read. Everyone talks about doing what the Holy Spirit says, but you do not state how you "know" it is the voice of God. I have yet to read any book or article that can lay that out. It is easy to say, "The Lord told me to leave this or do that, and I was blessed down the road because of it." Anyone who can present a way one can actually know that the voice they are hearing is from God, not man or Satan, would change the world. That's probably why the world hasn't changed.

I have good news—God wants to speak to us, and yes, you can "know" that you hear His voice. That "knowing" comes by exercising your spiritual ears and eyes. As the writer of Hebrews declares, we can train our ear to recognize the voice of God above all the noise of the other whispering voices:

> Solid food is for those who are mature, who through *training* have the skill to *recognize the difference between right and wrong.*
> —Hebrews 5:14, NLT, emphasis mine

It is by *practicing*, through *continual use* that we can discern whether what we are hearing is from God, the flesh, the world, or the Devil. What a comfort it is to know that—

with practice—we *can discern* what the voice of the Lord is saying:

> Your own ears will hear him. Right behind you a voice will say, "This is the way you should go," whether to the right or to the left.
> —Isaiah 30:21, NLT

What a tremendous promise this is for the believer!

Two-Way Communication

God wants to fellowship and communicate with you. That's two-way communication. Why? Because you can't have a relationship unless there is true dialogue. How do you get to know another person? By talking and listening.

It's the same with our relationship with God. He talks, we listen. We talk, He listens.

The book of Hebrews tells us that because of Jesus sacrifice on Calvary, God has given every believer access to His presence:

> And so, dear brothers and sisters, we can boldly enter heaven's Most Holy Place because of the blood of Jesus. This is the new, life-giving way that Christ has opened up for us through the sacred curtain, by means of his death for us.
> —Hebrews 10:19-20a, NLT

In the Garden of Eden, Adam and Eve had perfect, unhindered fellowship with God:

> They heard the sound of the LORD God walking in the Garden in the cool of the day.
> —Genesis 3:8, NASB

God wants to be that close and relate that intimately with us today. He wants to talk to us—and He wants us to listen and talk to Him, too.

The good news is that the Bible, God's revelation and love letter to mankind, makes it clear that we were created to have this kind of two-way communication with Him. As Jesus taught his disciples:

> My sheep hear My voice, and I know them, and they follow Me.
> —John 10:27, NASB

We don't have to walk blindly through life, wondering if we are making wise decisions. We can have confidence that we will hear our Father's voice. The Apostle Paul writes

> For all who are led by the Spirit of God are children of God.
> —Romans 8:14, NLT

If we are God's children, if we are truly born-again, the Holy Spirit will lead us through life.

God will order our steps, and even when we "blow it," if we are truly seeking to do His will, He will pick us up from where we have fallen and give us a second chance.

The most difficult part of hearing God is the time it takes to learn to discern God's voice from the many other voices that crowd our lives—and it takes a humble heart. Jeremiah 29:12-13 says:

> In those days when you pray, I will listen. If you look for me wholeheartedly, you will find me.
> —Jeremiah 29:12-13, NLT

If we want to learn how to hear God's voice then we have to do it His way. We can't make demands on Almighty God. We can't shake our fist at the sky and say, "All right God, what's the deal?" and expect to hear an answer. But we can ask, seek, and knock, and the Bible promises that God will open the door (Matthew 7:7). God will reveal Himself to those who humbly seek Him.

> Roll your works upon the Lord [commit and trust them wholly to Him; He will cause your thoughts to become agreeable to His will, and] so shall your plans be established and succeed.
>
> —Proverbs 16:3 AMPC

The Lord will reveal Himself to us, and through us, as we humbly seek Him. This familiar passage from Proverbs 3 makes this clear:

> Trust in the Lord with all your heart; do not depend on your own understanding. Seek his will in all you do, and he will show you which path to take.
>
> —Proverbs 3:6-7, NLT

God will speak, and you can hear His voice, but you must be careful—especially when you are a young Christian—that you seek ways to objectively confirm that you are following the Holy Spirit and not another voice. Our own flesh can scream pretty loud, especially when we are under pressure, or we want something very badly. The world can also be seductive. And the Devil is the father of lies—he is the great deceiver.

But God has provided a road map to help guide us into His plan for our lives!

The Seven Keys—An Overview

Let's look more closely at these seven basic keys or filters:

1. Scripture

Every possible leading, every prophetic word, every voice that we hear or sermon from the pulpit must line up with God's Word. The Bible must be the first and foremost plumb line for all that we do in life. Throughout recorded history, a *plumb line* has been used in building projects. A plumb line is a long piece of string that is weighted at one end, and when held from above it indicates a perfectly straight line. Scripture is to be the ultimate "plumb line" in our lives, the measuring rod against which everything must be lined up. Paul writes:

> All Scripture is inspired by God and is useful to teach us what is true and to make us realize what is wrong in our lives. It corrects us when we are wrong and teaches us to do what is right. God uses it to prepare and equip his people to do every good work.
> —2 Timothy 3:16-17, NLT

God will never contradict His Word. This is a great assurance as we seek His guidance. And we only know what is truly right and wrong based on God's revelation to us from the Scripture.

2. The Holy Spirit Speaking to our Heart

As we have already seen, God speaks to His children, and we can hear His voice—which is part of the covenant we have with God as New Testament believers.

> For this is the covenant that I will make with the house of Israel after those days, says the Lord: I will put my laws into their minds, and I will write them upon their hearts. And I will be their God, and they shall be my people. And they shall not teach everyone his fellow citizen, and everyone his brother, saying, 'know the Lord,' for all shall know Me, from the least to the greatest of them.
>
> —Hebrews 8:10-11, NASB

People who don't understand the ways of God might scoff and belittle the fact that you can hear His voice—but that doesn't make it any less true. In our post-modern world, those who would ridicule spirituality are quickly becoming the minority. The difficulty in the coming days will not be with modern thinkers who deny the spiritual realm because they can't explain it in scientific terms. Instead, the challenge will be confronting post-modern, "New Age" thinking that subscribes to "smorgasbord spirituality"—the idea that everyone can hear God, and each person can choose which god they prefer to listen to. "Best of all," proponents of these ideas say, "you can become a god yourself, while taking cues from the other gods of the universe."

Yikes—concepts like these are all too common today, and that is why we can't be led only by what we perceive to be the voice of God. We must balance any potential guidance with the other six keys. But rest assured, if you are truly seeking Almighty God—the God of the Bible—and are humble in your heart, He will direct your steps.

3. Godly Counsel

> Without wise leadership, a nation falls; there is safety in having many advisers.
> —Proverbs 11:14, NLT

We need each other. No one is able to fully comprehend the leading of God on their own because we all have our weaknesses. My father calls them "blind spots," and we all have them. Cindy Jacobs refers to them as the "hook in the jaw." These are the places where we are vulnerable to deception.

Thank God for the Body of Christ! As we walk together, we can receive counsel and direction from one another that comes from the Spirit of God. The Apostle Paul speaks of this in his letter to the church in Corinth:

> A spiritual gift is given to each of us so we can help each other...Yes, there are many parts, but only one body. The eye can never say to the hand, "I don't need you." The head can't say to the feet, "I don't need you."
> —1 Corinthians 12:7, 20-21, NLT

We need to be humble and willing to receive and prayerfully consider input from those leaders that God places in our lives.

The writer of Hebrews encourages us to:

> Remember those who led you, who spoke the word of God to you; and considering the result of their conduct, imitate their faith.
> —Hebrews 13:7, NASB

-and-

> Obey your leaders and submit to them, for they keep watch over your souls as those who will give an account.
> —Hebrews 13:17a, NASB

These are pretty strong words—but what I believe God is saying is to make sure that along with seeking to hear the voice of the Holy Spirit in prayer, we should also seek to hear Him through the godly leaders in our lives. The obedience is to Christ, but it is Jesus who speaks through these pastors and mentors that He places in your life. These are people of faith with whom you have a trusting relationship. It's not wise to open the circle of our most intimate friendships too wide—but neither is it spiritually-healthy to keep all things about our walk with the Lord to ourselves. We should seek mature men and women of God who will act as sounding boards for the direction we believe we're hearing from the Lord. Such advisors could include your spouse, your father or mother, your pastor or priest, a cell-group leader, your brother or sister—anyone who has demonstrated a proven track record of hearing God's voice and walking as a mature believer. They should be known for their walk of love, their wisdom, and for demonstrating the genuine fruit of the Spirit on an on-going basis in their lives.

4. The Peace of God

> Let the peace of Christ rule in your hearts, to which indeed you were called in one body; and be thankful.
> —Colossians 3:15, NASB

The Amplified Bible says the peace of God acts as the "umpire" of our hearts—it tells us whether we are "safe" (in

God's will), or "out" (on our own). I have often heard it said, "When God appoints, He anoints. When He calls, He equips. And what He orders, He pays for." If you're like me, you want to know that it is God appointing, calling and ordering the steps of your life. Without God's appointment, there is no anointing. Apart from the call of God, there is no equipping. And if He doesn't order it, guess who pays for it! I have paid some pretty expensive bills for the choices I made that were not in God's plan. There were other times in my life when I stepped out ahead of God's timing—which is another expensive proposition.

One way to avoid missing God's direction is to check our "peace-ometer" when we are considering a decision.

5. Personal Prophecy (Word of Knowledge, Word of Wisdom)

Prophecy can be defined simply as God communicating His thoughts and desires to man through other people. Dr. Bill Hamon, a respected prophetic leader, gives this caution about the prophetic:

> Though personal prophecy can play an important role in helping Christians make decisions, it is by no means the only way the Holy Spirit uses to reveal God's will and way. Probably 90 percent of my decisions, major and minor, have been made without personal prophecy being the dominating or even motivating faction. But I have striven to make 100 percent of all my decisions based upon God's Word, will, and way. [5]

---

[5] Hamon, Bill. Prophets and Personal Prophecy. (Shippensburg, PA: Destiny Image Publishers) 32.

The Bible clearly tells us to be receptive to prophetic words:

> Do not quench the Spirit; do not despise prophetic utterances...
> —1 Thessalonians 5:19-20, NASB

But the very next verse tells us to be cautious in our approach to the prophetic:

> ...but examine everything carefully; hold fast to that which is good.
> —1 Thessalonians 5:21, NASB

The apostle has said something both explicitly and implicitly in this passage. The explicit word to us is that we should welcome the gift of prophecy in our lives. But the implicit message is that not every word we receive through prophecy is good—even the most well-intentioned person can allow what would be a pure word to be tainted. For that reason, Paul has exhorted us to "test every prophecy" and "hold on to what is good."

6. Confirmation

> By the mouth of two or three witnesses every fact may be confirmed.
> —Matthew 18:16, NASB

Confirmation is reassurance that we have heard from God and are on the right track in following His guidance. Confirmation can come in a thousand different ways—it's up to the Lord which way He chooses. It's wonderful to know that the Lord promises us that He will confirm His word to us, and so we should ask Him to do so for us—especially when we are facing major life decisions. The cool thing is that these confirmations are often the most dramatic and faith-confirming aspects of our Christian walk!

7. Circumstances/Timing

Circumstances should not be ignored, or magnified when seeking the will of God in our lives. An interesting portion of Scripture tells how God used circumstances to make a major impact on the life of the early church.

> After these things he (Paul) left Athens and went to Corinth. And he found a certain Jew named Aquila, a native of Pontus, having recently come from Italy with his wife Priscilla, because Claudius had commanded all the Jews to leave Rome. He came to them, and because he was of the same trade, he stayed with them and they were working; for by trade they were tent-makers.
> —Acts 18:1-3, NASB

This relationship between Paul, Aquila, and Priscilla—birthed because of circumstances—became one of the most strategic partnerships in the book of Acts.

I have discovered that many Christians are on either end of the spectrum with regard to their view of circumstances and God's guidance. Some newly-saved or less mature Christians are led entirely by circumstances and completely ignore the other six keys. Then there are those "spooky spiritual" believers who completely ignore the circumstances of life because they claim to have heard the voice of God. They don't check this guidance against the other six keys, so they don't seem to care that there isn't enough money in their account to cover the "faith check" they just wrote.

If we will properly weigh circumstances—including God's timing—along with the other keys of God's guidance, we will see God bring tremendous spiritual fruit to our lives.

Many times the Lord will confirm His direction to us through several of these keys—especially when we are making important, life-changing decisions. But as we are learning about how God leads our steps, it's important to understand that His guidance won't always be spectacular. In fact, the majority of the time we may not even recognize God working in our lives until we look back and see how He orchestrated His plan. Some Christians are constantly looking for a supernatural display of some kind through dreams, visions, prophecies, angels, or voices. While these are all ways that God can, and sometimes does lead His people, most of the guidance from God occurs when we're not even conscious of it.

The Lord will direct the circumstances of our lives to move us here and there as He desires. He will also plant His desires in our hearts. We may think it is merely our own good idea. When we get to heaven, I think we're going to be amazed at how often the Lord directed our steps when we weren't even aware of it.

Denzel Washington shared this inspirational concept in a graduation speech he gave at Dillard University in New Orleans:

> Say thank you in advance for what's already yours. It's how I live my life. True desire, in the heart, for anything good, is God's proof to you sent beforehand to indicate that it's yours already. I'll say it again. True desire in the heart—that itch that you have ... that thing that you want to do to

help others, and to grow, and to make money—that desire, that itch, that's God's proof to you sent beforehand already to indicate that it's yours.

And anything good that you want, you can have. So claim it. Work hard to get it. When you get it, reach back, pull someone else up. Each one, teach one. Don't just aspire to make a living. Aspire to make a difference.[6]

When you study the cases of obvious guidance in the Bible, you discover that often when the Lord used some spectacular means of direction it was for the purpose of adjusting or correcting the direction in which His children were heading. I have found that God's guidance often seems like a natural occurrence any given day. It is not until I looked back over a period of time that I discovered, "Praise God, He truly does order my steps!"

We can also be confident that God will, from time-to-time, intervene in our lives to keep us from messing up His plan—as long as our hearts are right before Him, and we are truly seeking to be obedient to His will.

The bottom line is that big decisions require big prayer. But as we humble ourselves before the Lord and seek His guidance in our lives, the Good Shepherd will be faithful to lead us,

> He renews my strength. He guides me along right paths, bringing honor to his name.
> —Psalm 23:3, NLT

---

[6] Washington, Denzel. Commencement Speech, Dillard University, New Orleans, LA, 2015.

The New Testament talks of the early disciples—people like Paul, Aquila and Priscilla—as those who heard the voice of God. My friend who wrote the e-mail will be happy to know that this was the report made of the early church:

> ...These who have turned the world upside down have come here too.
>
> —Acts 17:6, NKJV

Yes, my friend, you can hear and know the voice of God. And because of this the world is changing ... more than perhaps you've heard.

Questions for Meditation

1. What do each of these passages have to teach us about hearing God's voice and discerning His will?

   > For all who are led by the Spirit of God are children of God.
   >
   > —Romans 8:14, NLT

   > In those days when you pray, I will listen. If you look for me wholeheartedly, you will find me.
   >
   > —Jeremiah 29:12-13, NLT

   > Your own ears will hear him. Right behind you a voice will say, "This is the way you should go," whether to the right or to the left.
   >
   > —Isaiah 30:21, NLT

   > My sheep listen to my voice; I know them, and they follow me.
   >
   > —John 10:27, NLT

2. What does "following the voice of the Good Shepherd" mean to you?

3. Describe a time in your life when you either did or did not use Scripture as a basis for making an important decision. What was the result?

4. Describe a time in your life when you either did or did not use the leading of the Holy Spirit as a basis for making an important decision. What was the result?

5. Describe a time in your life when you either did or did not use confirmation as a basis for making an important decision. What was the result?

Chapter Three

Tuning Into God's Frequency

Though we may not realize it, God is constantly communicating with us. The question you need to ask should be "am I tuned to His frequency?" Listening to the voice of the Lord is in some ways like tuning into a radio station. It may take some adjusting to get to the point where you are clearly hearing the signal from WGOD (or KGOD if you're from the western United States). What we need to realize is that God is on the other end, transmitting His message through the most powerful station in the universe—the Holy Spirit. By learning to adjust the spiritual knob through the seven keys you will mature to the point where you will be able to identify His signal and enjoy the sweet sound of His voice.

It might blow your mind to learn that God communicates with His people all day, every day. But just as a radio has to be turned on and tuned in, we must be available and listening—our ears tuned to His frequency to catch the signal He is sending.

So how do we tune in to WGOD?

In order to understand how God leads us today, a good place to start is to see how He has led his people and revealed Himself throughout history. Theologians would say that we need a proper understanding of general revelation, special revelation, and subordinate revelation. Let's take a brief look at these three ways God has revealed Himself in the past, and how they might apply to our lives today.

General Revelation

God has chosen to reveal Himself to mankind because of His love for us. Any knowledge that we have of God and His ways comes only because He has revealed it to us. God is the One who gives the revelation of Himself as He wills — when, where, why, how and to whom He wills.

Without this revelation, we would have no idea what is right or wrong. We would not know how to live or how to treat one another. His revelation is truly a gift of grace and love.

As C. S. Lewis put it:

> When you come to knowing God, the initiative lies on His side. If He does not show Himself, nothing you can do will enable you to find Him. And, in fact, He shows much more of Himself to some people than to others — not because He has favorites, but because it is impossible for Him to show Himself to a man whose whole mind and character are in the wrong condition. Just as sunlight,

though it has no favorites, cannot be reflected in a dusty mirror as clearly as a clean one. [7]

So too, God's revelation comes to those with a clean heart before Him.

It is first through the creation of the universe that God has chosen to reveal Himself to every human being. This is referred to as *general revelation.*

> For ever since the world was created, people have seen the earth and sky. Through everything God made, they can clearly see his invisible qualities—his eternal power and divine nature. So they have no excuse for not knowing God.
> —Romans 1:20, NLT

Sadly, some people see the wonder of creation but still refuse to believe in the Creator. In its fallen state, mankind doesn't want to believe what is clearly seen. But for those who walk in humility, nature is like an enormous cathedral filled with the presence of Almighty God.

The creation of the universe is not the only way in which God is revealed. Since human beings are made in the image and likeness of God, he or she is a mirror or reflection of God, who has written His moral law onto our hearts. Around the world we see people who worship, pray, build temples, shrines, and other places of worship. Throughout recorded time, man has searched for meaning in life and for the existence of God. It seems that God has planted a curiosity

---

[7] Lewis, C. S. *Mere Christianity* (New York: Touchstone, 1943), p. 144.

for things eternal into the hearts of men as a means of drawing them to Himself.

God is also revealed in the activities of man throughout history. Through the rise and fall of nations and peoples, God's hand can be seen time and time again. We recognize God's righteousness in the judgment or blessing of nations as they either reject or revere God.

Special Revelation

In His love and grace, God has chosen to reveal Himself to man through the people of the Bible—and primarily through His chosen people, the Jews. Theologian Dr. J. Rodman Williams writes:

> God has come to be known through His dealings with the people of the Scriptures. This was an ongoing, unfolding, evolving revelation of God in biblical history. He was revealed as the same holy and loving God throughout— He is never changing. But mankind is growing in our understanding of who God is as He reveals more and more to us in each generation—with an ever deepening and enlarging declaration of both His holiness and His love. [8]

This ongoing revelation of God through the Scriptures is called *special revelation.* God's special revelation of Himself began through the holy men and women who prophesied in the Old Testament. It's important to understand that under the Old Covenant the Holy Spirit did not indwell any person on a continual basis because mankind had not yet been

---

[8] Williams, J. Rodman. *Renewal Theology: God, the World, and Redemption* (Grand Rapids: Zondervan, 1988) 37.

redeemed from the fall. So the Lord chose special individuals—primarily the prophets of Israel—and the spirit of the Lord descended upon them to reveal the love and grace of God to the world.

The last of these Old Testament prophets was John the Baptist who announced the coming of the Lamb of God who would take away the sins of the world. And so the climax of God's personal revelation is Jesus Christ Himself. In Him:

> ...the Word became flesh and made His dwelling among us.
>
> —John 1:14, NIV

Jesus was God in the flesh, come to earth in fulfillment of two thousand years of Jewish history, precisely as foretold by the prophets. He showed mankind what God is like so we could know Him.

In the person of Jesus Christ, God, in the flesh, became known to the people of earth. Jesus Himself declared,

> ...Anyone who has seen me has seen the Father!
> —John 14:9, NLT

Jesus affirmed the full authority of the Old Testament as Scripture, but He made his own words and deeds equally authoritative.

Before He returned to heaven, Jesus promised His apostles that the Holy Spirit would remind them of his ministry and teach them its significance. So the New Testament apostles are the third venue of special revelation. These early Church leaders provided their special witness, declaring the whole counsel of God from the New Covenant perspective. Through this apostolic witness God's special revelation was canonized in the Bible in its final form.

At the Synod of Hippo in 393 AD, the Church fathers listed the 27 books of the New Testament after a long, drawn-out debate. The five general questions that were asked before a New Testament book was added were:

- Is it authoritative?
- Is it prophetic?
- Is it authentic?
- Is it dynamic?
- Did the people of God use it?

After reviewing their usage and authority, the council concluded that these books were already recognized as having authority in the Church, and so the canon was closed, giving us the New Testament Scriptures as we know them today.

The canon of the New Testament consists, then, of the authoritative record and interpretation of God's self-revelation by Jesus Himself. As Robert H. Gundry explains,

> The closing of the Canon by limiting it to apostolic books arose out of the recognition that God's revelation in Christ needs no improvement. [9]

---

[9] Gundry, Robert H. *A Survey of the New Testament* (Grand Rapids: Zondervan, 1994) 87.

Subordinate Revelation

In the New Testament Church today, God reveals Himself to the Christian community in a manner that is secondary to the Scriptures. This is done for the strengthening of the Church—to equip believers in their personal walk with the Lord and to empower them to take the Gospel to the ends of the earth. God has given the Church ongoing revelation as a part of the New Covenant. This revelation is given through the manifestation of the Holy Spirit—to our hearts and through the gifts of the Spirit.

As C. S. Lewis put it:

> The one really adequate instrument for learning about God is the whole Christian community, waiting for Him together. Christian brotherhood is, so to speak, the technical equipment for this science—the laboratory outfit.[10]

The coming of the Holy Spirit, the birth of the Church, and the writing of the Bible did not eliminate the need for the prophetic voice of the Lord; in fact, it intensified that need. The apostle Paul emphasized this truth when he told the church at Corinth to "covet to prophesy" (1 Corinthians 14:39, KJV).

It must always be understood that prophets and prophecy are not on the same level as the Scriptures. Prophecy provides illumination and it gives specific direction to the believer for a particular situation—it does not,

---

[10] Lewis, C. S. Mere Christianity. (New York: Touchstone, 1943) 145.

however, provide any further revelation than what the Bible has already given.

The ideal means of communication is God speaking directly to the heart of each individual by His Spirit and through the Scripture. However, even this guidance needs to be confirmed in the mouths of two or three witnesses—something that prophecy and the other keys can do.

Prophecy should never be a substitute for people seeking to hear God's voice for themselves. Yet many will not take time to listen for the voice of God. Others are under so much emotional strain when faced with an important decision that they aren't sure if they're hearing the voice of the Lord or not. Personal prophecy, including the word of knowledge and the word of wisdom, is a means for God to communicate with these people to bring edification, exhortation and comfort (1 Corinthians 14:3).

Later we will more thoroughly examine the role that prophets and prophecy play in the life of a Christian, but for now it is good to remember:

> To each is given the manifestation of the Spirit for the common good.
>
> —1 Corinthians 12:7, NLT

In other words, the Holy Spirit can and will manifest Himself through any willing believer who has faith.

The Great Adventure

"This is one of the greatest adventures of my life!" my then 8-year-old daughter, Margo, exclaimed almost breathlessly as we trekked along the narrow ledge of Wintergreen Gorge—one of Pennsylvania's awe-inspiring canyons.

Carved into the earth underneath the grinding weight of an ancient glacier, this lush valley is a spectacle of God's creativity and wonder. My breath was taken away when I stood at the base of the 100-foot sheer rock face cliffs observing eons of time reflected in the sedimentary layers that flow like tapestry across the canyon walls. I was filled with joy as I followed the delicate artistry of the channels in the bedrock where thousands of years of trickling water eroded ribbons of limestone in varying shapes and depths.

I was taken back to a simpler "Rockwellian time" as I watched my children frolic beneath a pristine waterfall. I remembered my own childhood with sentimental satisfaction as I helped my son, David, catch a salamander—and then I returned to my role as father as I urged him to set it free because it would be happier in the gorge.

I love hiking with my children through this living museum of natural curiosities. Of course, we never returned home without several pounds of souvenir rocks, fossils, and sometimes even the living critters that I couldn't save from David's bug box.

As we have already seen, Romans chapter one speaks of how God reveals Himself to mankind through the beauty of the earth. My thoughts are always sent heavenward when I experience nature—especially in places of grandeur like Wintergreen Gorge.

As we hiked along the valley floor we were constantly on the lookout for places to cross the meandering stream. While I was concerned about where I was placing my foot for the next step, working to keep from slipping into "the drink," I was also looking up from time-to-time to see where the best path would be ahead. I had to be vigilant so we could continue along our pathway without getting stranded between the steep walls and the flowing creek. On occasion we found ourselves in a place that had no narrow crossing. We had no choice but to gather large boulders and build a bridge to the other side of the waterway.

This constant action of looking down at my feet, and then up again at the trail ahead of me reminded me of the words of King David in the Psalms:

> Your word is a lamp to guide my feet and a light for my path.
> —Psalm 119:105, NLT

As Christians, our walk with the Lord is similar to this hike through Wintergreen Gorge. We need God's word for today to shine a light on the footsteps right before us—words of encouragement, comfort, wisdom, and sometimes, immediate direction for our safety, to keep us out of "the drink."

But we also need to have God's word to be a light for the path out in front of us. These are words of direction by the Holy Spirit, spoken to our hearts, through the ministry of a trusted godly friend, or even, perhaps, through the utterance of a prophet of God.

As the children and I built one of our stone bridges to get across the deep water I was reminded of a vision the Lord gave me during a time of decision in my life. I was facing some important choices and I felt the Lord leading me to fast and pray. During one of these prayer times I saw a picture in my spirit.

I was standing on the banks of the Niagara River, only a few short feet away from the edge of the falls. Stretched out before me were several large, flat boulders that rose out of the water, creating a dry and relatively safe bridge across. The only difficulty in navigating this bridge was that the rocks were spaced two-to-three feet apart—just far enough that it required a slight leap to get from one rock to the next. Below me the mighty Niagara raged, lapping up on the sides of the great boulders, and then thundering over the edge, hundreds of feet to the gorge below. God spoke to my heart that my task was to get to the other side of the river.

Although I was nervous about the rushing rapids, I was confident enough in my ability to leap from stone to stone. Gathering my courage, I leapt from the bank onto the first boulder, waving my arms as I landed to maintain my balance. The spray of the falls shot up in my face, and the thunder of the torrent rang in my ears, but I was safe for the moment on the first rock. Taking a minute to catch my breath and assess the situation I determined that this would not be as difficult as I had first imagined. Bounding forward I jumped to the next rock, and then to the next.

I was starting to get the hang of this, and suddenly I was feeling more confident than I should have. The pride of my accomplishment was crowding out the wisdom of caution that had earlier reigned in my heart. In that moment I forgot about God's plan in this scenario as I was caught up in the excitement of this "extreme sport"—crossing Niagara Falls.

But at that moment God did something that caught my attention. Just as I reached the middle of the river, poised to take my next jump, all of the daylight disappeared and I found myself standing there in the dead of night. I could still feel the spray of the water on my face, and now the roar of the waterfall echoed in my ears. I was overcome with the terror of my perilous circumstance. Suddenly I looked down and noticed that the stone I was standing on was lit, seemingly from within. The light shot up to my knees, and outward to illuminate the water rushing past me in an endless parade.

My thoughts turned to the Lord and I prayed, "Father, what are you showing me?"

He spoke gently to my spirit, "My child, Jesus is the rock that you are standing on, and the Holy Spirit is giving you the light of revelation for the place where you are. As long as you stay in the light, standing on the rock, you will be safe."

"But Lord," I inquired, "You called me to the other side of the river. How am I going to get across? I can't see your path before me."

Again the Lord spoke: "Don't move until I light up the next stone. You cannot leap into the darkness, hoping to land on a solid place. If you try to move forward in your own strength you will miss the rock, fall into the river, and be carried over the falls to disaster. In my time I will provide the light for your path."

I stood on that rock for a moment, listening to the torrents of water crashing onto the jagged boulders over the edge of the falls. But inside I finally had peace. I had the word of the Lord.

After a short time the rock in front of me lit up. "Go forward," the Lord spoke into my ear. With an easy leap I jumped onto that solid boulder, well above the raging river. As soon as I had landed safely on this new place the glow from the former stone disappeared, and only the light at my foot remained.

"This will be your life," the Lord declared as the vision dissipated. "You will walk a difficult path. Danger will lap at your feet beneath you. If you move out in your own strength you will risk being swept over the falls. You must stand on the rock, which is Jesus Christ. You must remain in fellowship with Me, and you must study and meditate on My word. I will provide a lamp for your feet, and a light for your path. Trust me completely, and only move forward when I light up the next stone."

I have been reminded of this vision from the Lord many times since that day as I have gone to the Lord in prayer for direction in my life—sometimes seeking a lamp for my foot in a particular day or circumstance, and sometimes desiring a light for my path to receive direction for the future.

In many ways my life has been like our hike through Wintergreen Gorge. I am constantly looking down at my feet, and then up again at the path ahead of me, all the time praying that God will direct my steps. But the Lord has always been faithful to guide me as I wait for His direction and timing.

The great church leader John Wesley said,

> Do not hastily ascribe all things to God. Do not easily suppose dreams, voices, impressions, visions, or revelations to be from God. They may be from Him, they

may be from nature, and they may be from the devil. Therefore, believe not every spirit but try the spirits, whether they be from God. [11]

Hearing from God doesn't have to be a mystical "spooky" thing. God gave us a brain and the ability to reason. He wants us to gather all the information we can and then make wise choices using our intellect in submission to His Spirit. We gather that information through the seven keys that are presented in this study. The wonderful promise from Scripture is that if we are willing to submit to God, and we ask Him to lead our steps, He will be faithful to do it! And even if we miss it now and then, He will get us back on the right track as we humbly obey Him and follow His leading.

Dr. Richard Dobbins writes,

> You need to see God's will as a stream. You can step into and out of a stream. I know many people who see the will of God as a road that comes to a fork. If you take the wrong path at the fork, they say you can never get back into the will of God. I would rather see God's will as a stream.
>
> At times you may step out and when you step out of it, you are going to miss the refreshing of that stream. The fact that you are out of it does not mean you cannot get back into it. Ask God to give you a fascination and an urge to go down the way that represents His will for you.[12]

God's guidance comes step by step, incrementally in life. Taking the first step puts us in the position to take the next

---

[11] Mumford, Bob. *Take Another Look at Guidance* (Plainfield, NJ: Logos, 1971) preface.
[12] Dobbins, Dr. Richard. "Seeking god's Will," DayForward Online, 2002.

step after that. I agree with Margo's assessment of this journey of faith, *it is one of the greatest adventures of my life!*

Are you passionate about discovering and obeying God's will for your life? Do you want to see God's kingdom established in the world? Do you want to learn how to hear the voice of God? Do you want to know how to employ the seven keys of God's guidance in every decision in your life? Then read on.

Questions For Meditation

1. Have you seen the general revelation of God in your own heart and life?

2. How has God been revealed to you in nature? ...in His creation of man? ...throughout history?

3. How has God revealed Himself to you through His Word, the Bible?

4. How was God revealed to mankind in the person of Jesus Christ?

5. Has His direction ever been confirmed to you through another Christian? Explain.

6. How has God's Word been a lamp to your feet—the immediate decisions that you need to make?

7. How has it been a light to your path—the future direction for your life?

Chapter Four

The Scriptures - God Speaks Through His Inspired Word

*A*s my children were growing up we had a time of prayer together every morning before they left for school and I went off to work. The key element of that prayer was to put on the armor of God that the Apostle Paul speaks of in Ephesians 6. As we prayed, each of us would take a turn with a different part of the armor. When it was time to take up the sword that person prayed, "We take up the sword of the Spirit, which is the Word of God, to fight back against the enemy." Then I would ask in a loud voice, "And what do we say?" And the whole family would cry out, "It is written!"

The phrase *it is written* is taken from the gospel account of Jesus being tempted by Satan:

> Then Jesus was led by the Spirit into the wilderness to be tempted there by the devil. For forty days and forty nights he fasted and became very hungry.
>
> During that time the devil came and said to him, "If you are the Son of God, tell these stones to become loaves of bread."
>
> But Jesus told him, "No! The Scriptures say, 'People do not live by bread alone, but by every word that comes from the mouth of God.'"
>
> Then the devil took him to the holy city, Jerusalem, to the highest point of the Temple, and said, "If you are the Son of God, jump off! For the Scriptures say, 'He will order his angels to protect you. And they will hold you up with their hands so you won't even hurt your foot on a stone.'"
>
> Jesus responded, "The Scriptures also say, 'You must not test the Lord your God.'"
>
> Next the devil took him to the peak of a very high mountain and showed him all the kingdoms of the world and their glory. "I will give it all to you," he said, "if you will kneel down and worship me."
>
> "Get out of here, Satan," Jesus told him. "For the Scriptures say, 'You must worship the Lord your God and serve only him.'"
>
> Then the devil went away, and angels came and took care of Jesus.
>
> —Matthew 4:1-11, NLT

Every time Satan tried to tempt Him, Jesus answered by declaring, "It is written..." and then He quoted the key passage from the Old Testament to thwart Satan's temptation. Jesus used the Word of God as his weapon to fight back against the temptation of the Devil—and so must we.

Jesus succeeded where Adam and Eve failed. In the Garden of Eden, Satan, disguised as the serpent, brought three temptations to Adam and Eve. The serpent convinced them first that the forbidden tree was good for food. Second, he told them that it was pleasant to the eyes. And finally he deceived them into believing that it was a tree desirable to make one wise. In the New Testament, the apostle John warned not to be tempted by these things of the world, and called them the lust of the flesh, the lust of the eyes, and the pride of life (1 John 2:16).

- The lust of the flesh—the forbidden fruit was good for food;

- The lust of the eyes—the forbidden fruit was pleasant to the eyes;

- The pride of life—the forbidden fruit would make them wise.

Jesus, who is called the last Adam by the apostle Paul (1 Corinthians 15:45), overcame the same three temptations that Satan used against the first Adam:

- The lust of the flesh—turn the stones into bread to feed the flesh;

- The lust of the eyes—*see* all the kingdoms of the world and their glory;

- The pride of life—throw yourself down from the pinnacle of the temple and the angels will catch you and preserve your life.

Jesus Christ is our example of how to live this life, and He used the Word of God to defeat Satan in this time of temptation. That is why I taught my children to boldly declare in the face of temptation or danger that "It is written…" The writer of Hebrews speaks of the power of God's word in our lives.

> For the word of God is alive and powerful. It is sharper than the sharpest two-edged sword, cutting between soul and spirit, between joint and marrow. It exposes our innermost thoughts and desires.
> —Hebrews 4:12, NLT

Jesus told his disciples that He spoke only what the Father wanted Him to speak (John 12:49). So when He quoted these Old Testament passages to Satan, Jesus was speaking from the authoritative Scriptures. In other words, Jesus was confirming that the Old Testament is God's Holy Word.

Christians believe and teach that the Bible is inspired by the Holy Spirit—God spoke these words to men who faithfully wrote them down and gave them to the world. The Scripture—Old and New Testament—is the final authority for our faith and life. The Holy Bible—or as theologians would call it, the canon of Scripture—is the guiding truth for all believers.

Building Our Trust in God's Word

The apostle Paul spoke of this in his second letter to Timothy:

> You have been taught the holy Scriptures from childhood, and they have given you the wisdom to receive the salvation that comes by trusting in Christ Jesus. All Scripture is inspired by God and is useful to teach us what is true and to make us realize what is wrong in our lives. It corrects us when we are wrong and teaches us to do what is right.
>
> —2 Timothy 3:15-16, NLT

Of the seven keys of God's guidance, the Scriptures are paramount. It has been said that 95 percent of all the guidance we need as Christians can be found in the clearly understood principles of the Holy Bible. It is the standard by which every doctrine can be judged. Any guidance we receive must line up with the Word of God, or it must be rejected outright.

That is why a study of the seven keys must begin with a clear understanding that the Bible is God's infallible word. The Bible is our guide in life, and so we need to know how to properly read and interpret it.

A non-believer may respond, "Hey, why are you so narrow minded? What makes your holy book more special than any other holy book? How is the Bible different than the Qur'an, or the Book of Mormon, or any other book that claims to be God's word?"

The Christian view of the Bible is that it isn't just a holy book—it is the inspired revelation from God. If it is truly the final word from God, then there can be no other book that could be God's word.

The word *inspired* in 2 Timothy 3:16 is translated from the Greek word *theopnuestos*, which literally means *God-*

breathed. Some theologians translate this word as "esspired," or "breathed out." In other words, God breathed forth his Word to mankind. He didn't just stir the imaginations of the writers who then wrote something that touches on God's leading, as some Bible critics have said. The Holy Spirit inspired the writers of Scripture in such a way that they wrote precisely what God wanted to communicate.

While some things were "dictated" to the writers, like the Law of Moses and the Ten Commandments for example, in many other cases the Holy Spirit divinely guided the choice of words they used. Dr. Jimmy Williams writes: "...for the most part, the Spirit simply superintended the writing so that the writer, using his own words, wrote what the Spirit wanted written." [13]

Evidence from the Old Testament

The Old Testament explicitly states 3,808 times that it is conveying God's very words.[14]

The Jews in Old Testament times considered the Law of Moses to be the true Word of God. They felt such awe and respect toward Scripture that they worked with almost fanatical discipline to preserve the unblemished accuracy of the documents. In ancient times, no printing presses existed. Instead, professional people known as scribes were trained to meticulously copy documents. These devout laborers

---

[13] Williams, Jimmy. *Evidence, Answers, and Christian Faith* (Grand Raids: Kregel, 2002) 95.
[14] Rene Pache, *The Inspiration and Authority of Scripture* (Chicago: Moody, 1969) 81.

believed they were entrusted with the authentic Word of God, and so they approached their duties with extreme discipline and precision.

All of the earliest copies of the Hebrew Scriptures are in remarkable agreement. This was confirmed when a discovery of monumental proportions happened by accident in 1947. A young Bedouin goatherd was exploring some hot, dry caves near the Dead Sea when he stumbled upon some ancient clay jars. Inside these jars were scrolls of papyrus, leather, and copper—the now famous Dead Sea Scrolls.

Found in eleven different caves from 1947 to 1956, the discoveries include a complete copy of the book of Isaiah; a fragmented copy of Isaiah, which contains much of Isaiah 38-66; and references to every book in the Old Testament except Esther. The majority of the fragments are from Isaiah and the Pentateuch (Genesis, Exodus, Leviticus, Numbers and Deuteronomy). Fragments of the books of Samuel were found along with two complete chapters of the book of Habakkuk. There is agreement among most scholars that these materials were written during the last centuries of the second temple, from 200 B.C. to A.D. 100.

As scholars examined the Dead Sea Scrolls, and compared them to the Masoretic Text copied a thousand years later, they made an amazing discovery—they are virtually identical.

In his book *Know Why You Believe*, Paul Little writes

> A comparison of Isaiah 53 shows that only 17 letters differ from the Masoretic Text. Ten of these are mere differences in spelling (like [American] "honor" and the English "honour") and produce no change in the meaning

at all. Four more are very minor differences, such as the presence of a conjunction (and) which are stylistic rather than substantive. The final three letters are the Hebrew word for *light*. This word was added to the text by someone after *they shall see* in verse 11. Out of 166 words in this chapter, only this one word is really in question, and it does not at all change the meaning of the passage."[15]

Evidence from the New Testament

The writers of the New Testament also verified the validity of the Bible as the Word of God. The apostle Paul declared that His teachings came to Him as a direct revelation from Christ. Peter described the writing of Paul as revelation from God, like "the other Scriptures" (2 Peter 3:16). Jimmy Williams in his book *Evidence, Answers, and Christian Faith* writes that the Greek word *graphe* in the New Testament refers only to sacred Scriptures. *Graphe* was used in 1 Timothy 5:18 and 2 Peter 3:16 to refer to the writings of the apostles.[16]

Archaeological and Literary Evidence

So, how do we know that the Bible we have today is like the original message of the writers?" In his book *More Than a Carpenter*, Josh McDowell shares the story of a confrontation with a professor over the reliability of the New Testament:

---

[15] Paul Little, *Know Why You Believe* (Downer's Grove, Ill." InterVarsity, 1968) 41.
[16] Williams, Jimmy. *Evidence, Answers, and Christian Faith* (Grand Raids: Kregel, 2002) 84-85.

> The professor said, "Mr. McDowell, you are basing all your claims about Christ on a second-century document that is obsolete. I showed in class today how the New Testament was written so long after Christ that it could not be accurate in what it recorded."
>
> I replied, "Your opinions and conclusions about the New Testament are twenty-five years out of date."[17]

That professor's thoughts about the claims of Jesus originated with a German critic, F. C. Baur, who assumed that most of the New Testament Scriptures were not written until late in the second century A.D. He concluded that these writings came basically from myths or legends that had developed during the interval of time between the life of Jesus in the first century and when these writings were purportedly created.

But archaeological discoveries have proved him wrong. Many exciting archaeological breakthroughs happened in the twentieth century that confirmed the authenticity of the New Testament. The unearthing of early papyri manuscripts, including the John Ryland manuscript, A.D. 130; the Chester Beatty Papyri, ca. A.D. 155; and the Bodmer Papyri II, A.D. 200, bridged the gap between the time of Jesus and existing manuscripts from a later date.

Today, archaeologists have unearthed more than three thousand different, ancient Greek manuscripts containing all or portions of the New Testament. Biblical scholars of all persuasions around the world have come to an increased

---

[17] Josh McDowell, *More Than a Carpenter* (Wheaton, IL.: Tyndale House Publishers, 1977), p. 41-42.

confidence in the reliability of the Bible based on these exciting archaeological discoveries.

Yale Scholar Millar Burrows explained the significance of these discoveries:

> Another result of comparing New Testament Greek with the language of the papyri [discoveries] is an increase of confidence in the accurate transmission of the text of the New Testament itself. [18]

One of the leading archaeologists of all time, William Albright, dated the New Testament in the first century A.D.:

> We can already say emphatically that there is no longer any solid basis for dating any book of the New Testament after about A.D. 80, two full generations before the date between 130 and 150 given by the more radical New Testament critics of today.[19]

He further clarifies his position in an interview for *Christianity Today*.

> In my opinion, every book of the New Testament was written by a baptized Jew between the forties and the eighties of the first century A.D. (very probably sometime between about A.D. 50 and 75).[20]

Now that we know that we can trust the authenticity of the Bible, let's take a look at how we can best read, interpret, and apply the truths of God's Word to our lives.

---

[18] Burrows, Millar. *What Mean These Stones?* (New York: Meridian, 1956), 52.
[19] William F. Albright, *Recent Discoveries in Bible Lands* (New York: Funk and Wagnalls, 1955), p. 136.
[20] William F. Albright, *Christianity Today*, Vol. 7, Jan. 18, 1963, p. 3.

How to Read God's Word

In order to accurately judge the other keys of God's guidance against the Scriptures we must first learn how to properly read and interpret the Scriptures for ourselves.

Every believer should make it his or her goal to eventually read through the whole Bible. But if you are just starting out, you may want to approach the Scripture like a library of 66 mini-books. Start your reading with the Gospel of John, because the writer was one of the closest people to Jesus on the earth, and the book is written with many intimate details. Next read the book of Acts, which tells us how the disciples lived in the power of God's Holy Spirit. When you are finished, read the book of Romans, which clearly describes the great doctrines that Paul taught. Then read the letters of John, and Paul's epistle to the Philippians. Then go on to read the Old Testament stories of key people in the book of Genesis. After that, turn to the Psalms to learn what it means to worship God and pour out your inner feelings to Him, and then to Proverbs to discover His wisdom. You can continue from there until you have read the whole Bible, word for word.

- Gospel of John
- Acts
- Romans
- 1 John, 2 John, 3 John
- Philippians
- Genesis
- Psalms
- Proverbs

The next step is to learn how to interpret what you are reading in the Bible. One of the biggest mistakes many Christians make is to ascribe to Bible passages meaning that the original text never intended. The best way to approach Bible study is with a goal of discovering first what the biblical texts meant to the people for whom they were originally written. In other words, in order to apply meaning from the Scriptures for ourselves today, we must first discover what the meaning was for the readers then.

When studying the Bible we have two tasks: First, to find out what the text originally meant—this is called *exegesis*. Second, we must learn to hear that same meaning in the variety of new or different contexts of our own day—this is called *hermeneutics*. Many of the difficulties in the church today come as a result of the basic struggle with bridging the hermeneutical gap—moving from the "then and there" of the original text to the "here and now" of our own life settings.

In their book *How to Read the Bible for All Its Worth*, Gordon Fee and Douglas Stuart state:

> The aim of good interpretation is simple, to get at the "plain meaning of the text." And the most important ingredient one brings to that task is enlightened common sense. The first reason one needs to learn how to interpret is that, whether one likes it or not, every reader is at the same time an interpreter. That is, most of us assume as we read that we also understand what we read. We also tend to think that our understanding is the same thing as the Holy Spirit's or human author's intent. However, we invariably bring to the text all that we are, with all our experiences, culture, and prior understandings of words

and ideas. Sometimes what we bring to the text, unintentionally to be sure, leads us astray, or else causes us to read all kinds of foreign ideas into the text.[21]

For this reason, it's important to ask the right questions to find the original meaning of the text:

- What is the historical context of the book, including the time and culture of the author and the readers, as well as the geographical, topographical, and political factors that are relevant to the author's setting?

- What prompted its writing?

- What is the overall purpose of the book?

- What is the literary context of the wording?

- What is the "point" that the author is trying to make?

- What is the author saying, and why does he or she say it at that particular point in the text?

- What is the meaning of the words that have been chosen?

- What are the grammatical relationships in the sentences?

- When translations differ, what did the original text say?

After these basic questions have been answered, you can begin the task of hermeneutics: seeking the contemporary relevance of the ancient texts. When finding a modern application, it's important to be careful of pride and super-

---

[21] Fee, Gordon D. and Douglas Stuart. *How to Read the Bible for All Its Worth* (Grand Rapids: Zondervan, 1981), 11.

spirituality. The aim of interpretation is not uniqueness—you are not trying to discover what no one else has ever seen before. You are striving to apply God's eternal truth to your life.

This kind of inductive Bible study is not intended to take the joy from daily devotional reading of the Bible. In time, serious Bible study will actually enhance devotional reading because the principles and insights gained from this exercise will open up new and exciting understanding of the biblical text that will deepen and broaden your time in communication with your Heavenly Father.

One of the surest principles of biblical understanding is that Scripture interprets Scripture. If some passage is not clear in itself, often the most helpful procedure is to turn to other similar verses that may cast light on the one being considered. Such procedure obviously calls for a wide knowledge of the Bible, for the more comprehensive one's knowledge may be, the more able he will be to apply it to a given passage. It is also a good idea to invest in Bible interpretation software.

One of my professors in the School of Divinity at Regent University was asked what translation he preferred.

"The Greek," he answered with a serious expression as the student's chuckled.

"No, really," the student replied, "which translation do you read in your daily devotional time?"

"The Greek," the professor replied again, this time allowing the edges of his mouth to rise in a slight smile.

Any knowledge of Hebrew and Greek is of course valuable, since these are the original languages of the Old and New Testaments. But even if you are not able to read Hebrew or Greek, today there are many computer programs that provide valuable insight into the biblical languages.

In order to fully comprehend the Scriptures we need the help that can only come from other Christians. From the earliest days of the church, believers were strengthened in their faith by the teaching of Christian leaders. One of first things said about the believers after the day of Pentecost was that

> All the believers devoted themselves to the apostles' teaching...
> —Acts 2:42, NLT

Faithful attendance in a Bible believing church to receive anointed preaching and teaching, study of God's word together in Sunday School and home fellowships, the reading of good Bible commentaries, inductive Bible study—these are just some of the ways we can grow in our knowledge of God's written word.

Logos or Rhema

The great 18th Century church leader John Wesley said:

> We sought counsel from the oracles of God.[22]

By examining the Scriptures, Wesley and his followers believed they would be led by God. They looked at the written Word of God, known in the Greek as the *Logos*, and desired

---

[22] Wesley, John. *Preface to Explanatory Notes upon the Old Testament* (Edinburgh, April 28, 1765).

to receive a personal word of revelation our guidance, what the Greek calls a *rhema*.

The apostle John used the term *Logos* in relationship to Jesus Christ as the word made flesh (John 1:1, 14). As the *Logos*, both the Bible and Jesus are eternal, and they are one. The written word is a revelation of the Living Word. Theologians have said that the Bible is not simply one book God could have written, it is the only book, because it is a revelation of Himself, and there is only one revelation of God.

The *Logos* Word is given to all man—it is God's revelation to the world. But people must act upon the *Logos* in order to receive all from the Scriptures that God intended for them. As James writes,

> ...Faith without works is dead.
> —James 2:26, NASB

Millions of people own a Bible, and many may even read it, but it is meaningless without faith and corresponding action. For example, until a person acts in faith on the directive from God from Romans 10:9, "to confess with your mouth the Lord Jesus and believe in your heart that God has raised Him from the dead," there is no salvation.

> If you openly declare that Jesus is Lord and believe in your heart that God raised him from the dead, you will be saved.
> —Romans 10:9, NLT

This is true of every promise of the Scriptures. Unless we step out in faith to receive them as our own, they will be just like the lifeless family Bibles that sit unread on many people's dusty shelves.

Just as John Wesley received direction from the oracles of God, we can have the Bible come alive for us as we diligently read and study. The Lord will often speak to us out of the Scriptures by what is known as a *rhema*—a Holy Spirit-inspired Word from the *Logos* that brings life, power, and faith to perform and fulfill it.

God illuminates a personal revelation (*rhema*) for you from the general word (*Logos*) that He has given to all mankind. As you seek to know the Lord by reading His word, specific things may leap out of the pages and come to life. The Holy Spirit will quicken these truths to you—and this is one of the exciting ways God leads us through His Word.

That's why it is important to ask the Holy Spirit to guide you into the truth (John 16:13) when you sit down to study the Bible. This prayer is the starting point to understanding the Scriptures.

A *rhema* word must be evaluated by both the spirit and the context of the *Logos*. The *rhema* word is dependent upon the *Logos* just as a branch is dependent upon a vine.

Scripture interprets Scripture. You can stake your life, your future, your marriage, your health, your hope—everything—on God's Word! Just as we do with every form of guidance, when we believe God has revealed a *rhema* word to us from the Bible we must evaluate it against the other six keys.

Being Led Through the Scriptures

There is an unhealthy practice in seeking direction through the Scriptures that is sometimes called "Bible bingo." This occurs when someone who wants guidance from the Lord through the Scripture lets the Bible fall open and then points his finger at a verse, trusting that this will be the "word of the Lord" for them. The old joke about this practice is that a certain person first pointed at the verse that reads, Judas "...went away and hanged himself" (Matthew 27:5). Under the impression that God wanted to say more, this person pointed at another verse that said, "...go out and do likewise" (Luke 10:37b).

Seeking direction through Bible bingo, casting lots, or setting out "fleeces," are dangerous gambles with God's direction and should be avoided by the New Testament Christian. In the Old Testament, God sometimes guided his people through casting lots or setting out fleeces. But today God leads His people through His Word and by His Spirit.

There is a valid way of being led through the Scriptures that is different from Bible bingo, and that is when the Holy Spirit plants a verse in your heart or causes a portion of Scripture to jump off the page at you as you are reading. The Lord has often spoken amazing things to me through this method of Holy Spirit inspired direction through His Word—but as always, I confirmed this leading through the other keys.

Study to Show Yourself Approved

As Christians it is our responsibility and privilege to know the Word of God for ourselves. We can't rely on someone else's concept of Christianity to guide us. The Lord has made His Word available to us, and to whom much is given, much is required. You must study to know the Scriptures for yourself.

Great heroes of the faith have struggled, fought, and even died so that you and I could read the Bible. The Scriptures were not always as readily available as they are today. In the Middle Ages only the priest, royalty, the religious elite, and the extremely wealthy could read and have access to the Holy Scriptures. But through the courageous stand of such great men and Wycliffe, Huss, Luther, Tyndale, and others the Bible was made available to the common man in the common tongue.

You and I have a wonderful privilege that others in history only dreamed of—we have total access to the Word of God and can read and study it every day. As David wrote:

> O how I love Your law! It is my meditation all the day.
> —Ps. 119:97, NASB

I encourage you to make Bible study and meditational reading a priority in your life.

As we study and meditate on God's Word we can store away the principles that are gleaned to be drawn upon later when we are seeking specific guidance for our lives. God loves us so much that He made sure His Word was made available to us. He protected and passed it from generation to generation so we could have it as a guide and comfort for our lives. Remember, the Holy Spirit will never lead us contrary to His Word.

We need to be serious students of the Bible. The Lord will keep you in the center of His plan as you seek Him first and meditate on His Word on a daily basis. Psalm 1:1-3 gives us not only the directive to meditate on God's word daily, but also the results of making this discipline a part of our lives.

> Blessed is the man who walks not in the counsel of the ungodly, nor stands in the path of sinners, nor sits in the seat of the scornful; But his delight is in the law of the Lord, and in His law he meditates day and night. He shall be like a tree planted by the rivers of water that brings forth its fruit in its season, whose leaf also shall not wither, and whatever he does shall prosper.
> —Psalm 1:1-3, NKJV

To meditate is to think often about the character and the ways of God—of His teachings, principles, and the example of Jesus Christ on the Earth—and then to apply these truths to the circumstances of your life. As we read the Bible on a daily basis we must endeavor to apply the principles we find to the situations we encounter in that day. That's why Jesus taught us to pray:

> ...give us *this day* our *daily bread*...
> —Matthew 6:11, NASB, emphasis mine)

As you make Scripture reading and meditation a daily discipline, you open your soul to the influence of what you have read. As a result, you seek to be Christ-like in all you do. If this is your lifestyle, then your life will be opened in a dramatic way to the Lord's guidance.

And so the progression of God's adventure of faith goes in the life of a believer.

If you want guidance from the Lord, and if you want to recognize the voice of God, then get to know the Word of God through reading and meditating on the Scriptures. God is faithful to all His promises and He will never contradict Himself. Knowledge of the Bible will keep you from falling into deception and error.

Questions For Meditation

1. What does it mean to you that Scripture is God-breathed?

2. Read Matthew 5:17-19. How does this passage demonstrate Jesus' opinion of the Old Testament?

> Don't misunderstand why I have come. I did not come to abolish the law of Moses or the writings of the prophets. No, I came to accomplish their purpose. I tell you the truth, until heaven and earth disappear, not even the smallest detail of God's law will disappear until its purpose is achieved. So if you ignore the least commandment and teach others to do the same, you will be called the least in the Kingdom of Heaven. But anyone who obeys God's laws and teaches them will be called great in the Kingdom of Heaven.
> —Matthew 5:17-19, NLT

3. Read 2 Peter 3:15-16. According to what did Peter say Paul had written his letters? Why is this significant?

> And remember, our Lord's patience gives people time to be saved. This is what our beloved brother Paul also wrote to you with the wisdom God gave him—speaking of these things in all of his letters. Some of his comments are hard to understand, and those who are ignorant and unstable have twisted his letters to mean something quite different, just as they do with other parts of Scripture. And this will result in their destruction.
> —2 Peter 3:15-16, NLT

4. Has the archaeological evidence increased your trust in and reliance upon the Word of God? If so, how?

5. How can we be sure that we are reading the Bible "correctly"?

6. Describe a situation in your life in which the Bible clearly told you what decision you should make. What did you do? How did the situation turn out?

7. How does the original intent of the biblical author affect our interpretation of what is in the Bible?

8. Explain the difference between the *Logos* and a *rhema* word from God. How are the two interrelated?

9. How does the Holy Spirit-inspired direction through the Word differ from "Bible bingo"?

10. Re-read Psalm 1:1-3. In what does a "blessed" person delight? What does he or she do with the law of the Lord? What is the result?

> Oh, the joys of those who do not follow the advice of the wicked, or stand around with sinners, or join in with mockers. But they delight in the law of the Lord, meditating on it day and night.
>
> They are like trees planted along the riverbank, bearing fruit each season. Their leaves never wither, and they prosper in all they do.
>
> —Psalm 1:1-3, NLT

CHAPTER FIVE

THE LEADING OF THE HOLY SPIRIT - LEARNING TO RECOGNIZE GOD'S STILL, SMALL VOICE

Because God is a Spirit, He leads his people in the spirit. The Church described in the book of Acts was Spirit-led. In Acts chapter one, Jesus set the stage for the infant Church:

> ...you shall receive power *when the Holy Spirit has come upon you*; and *you shall be My witnesses* both in Jerusalem, and in all Judea and Samaria, and even to the remotest part of the earth.
> —Acts 1:8, NASB, emphasis mine

It is the Holy Spirit who is Emmanuel, God with us, and He empowers believers to be witnesses in the world.

It's interesting to observe that before the Holy Spirit descended on the disciples, an important decision was made by the Apostles. In obedience to Jesus' command, the disciples returned to the upper room in Jerusalem, devoting themselves to prayer and waiting for the promised Holy Spirit. At that time, Peter suggested that the place of Judas, one of the original twelve Apostles, needed to be filled, and the rest of the disciples agreed. In Acts 1:26 they cast lots and Matthias was selected to become the twelfth Apostle. There is not another occurrence of casting lots in the rest of the New Testament. While casting lots was common practice in the Old Testament, it's significant that it was never practiced again by the New Testament Christians after the day of Pentecost. Why? Because when the Holy Spirit came, He dramatically fulfilled Jesus promise to lead all believers into the truth! There was no more need for casting lots after the early disciples learned how to hear the voice of the Holy Spirit and follow His leading.

There are numerous examples of the Apostles following the leading of the Holy Spirit, but not another single example of casting lots. When the time came to send out the first missionaries from Antioch, the leadership did not resort to drawing straws or rolling dice. The Bible says:

> One day as these men were worshiping the Lord and fasting, *the Holy Spirit* said, "Appoint Barnabas and Saul for the special work to which I have called them."
> —Acts 13:2, NLT, emphasis mine

Notice that Luke writes, "the Holy Spirit said..." The God of the Bible is a personal God, not just some spiritual force in the universe. The Holy Spirit is a person—and in this case, that person spoke directly to the disciples and gave them specific direction for the early church.

Jesus Christ is the same yesterday, today and forever (Hebrews 13:8). There is no partiality with God (Romans 2:11). So if the Holy Spirit spoke to the disciples at Antioch, you can be confident that He is still speaking to the Church today!

Later, Saul would become Paul, and would write to the church in Rome, exhorting them to "walk in the Spirit" and not in the flesh. Throughout the book of Acts we see the disciples sent out like this into the world as the Spirit led them.

It's vital that we as Christians submit ourselves to the same leading today. If we want New Testament results, we need to use New Testament methods—and the most important thing we can do is to become sensitive to the voice of the Holy Spirit.

We see a dramatic biblical example of the life in the Spirit from Paul himself, beginning in Acts 20. Meeting with the elders in the church at Ephesus, Paul encourages them and then declares:

> And now, behold, *bound by the Spirit*, I am on my way to Jerusalem, not knowing what will happen to me there, except that *the Holy Spirit solemnly testifies to me* in every city, saying that bonds and afflictions await me.
> —Acts 20:22-23, NASB, emphasis mine

How did Paul know these things? Because he was living a dynamic Christian life, walking in the spirit by faith. "By reason of use..." he had become sensitive to the voice of the Holy Spirit so he was able to "...discern between good and evil" (Hebrews 5:14).

You and I can enjoy that same kind of life in the Spirit today! Jesus declared the kingdom of God is among us. We just need to take a step of faith to leave our safe, comfortable, spiritually-unproductive life in the flesh, and enter the unsure, uncomfortable, but exciting and fruit-bearing life in the spirit.

In verses 37 and 38, the Bible says the other believers,

> They all cried as they embraced and kissed him goodbye. They were sad most of all because he had said that they would never see him again. Then they escorted him down to the ship.
>
> —Acts 20:37-38, NLT

These early Christian were so confident in the leading of the Holy Spirit that when Paul said he would see them no more, they believed him—and it brought them to tears.

The story continues in Acts chapter 21 as Paul presses on toward Jerusalem. Stopping along the way in Tyre, he located the disciples and stayed with them for seven days. During his time with them, the disciples continued to tell Paul through the Spirit not to set foot in Jerusalem. Paul was unmovable. When his time in Tyre was over he thanked the disciples for their hospitality and boarded another ship for his final voyage towards Jerusalem.

Before entering Jerusalem, Paul visited the house of Philip the evangelist. The Bible tells us that this man had four virgin daughters who were prophetesses. After they stayed in the house for several days, a prophet named Agabus came down from Judea. Luke makes it quite clear that there were several people in the house who walked in the spirit and were sensitive to the voice of God. In verse 11, Agabus physically demonstrates the prophetic word he received from the Lord telling Paul he would be bound and imprisoned.

There it is again—it is the same word the disciples in Tyre had for Paul. Now remember, Agabus was no slouch. He was a respected prophet with a proven track record (See Acts 11:27-29). Agabus validated and confirmed the previous word that had come to Paul. When the disciples heard this, they begged Paul not to go to Jerusalem—again because they were confident that Agabus was hearing from God.

Paul had to make a decision at this point. Would he trust in the leading that he had received from the Spirit, or would he listen to the impassioned pleas of the other disciples? It may seem to us as if the word that he had heard directly from the Lord contradicted with the words from the other disciples—but that wasn't the case. The contradiction was not in the word of the Lord, but in *the different interpretations* of that word.

This is why it is vital to consider all seven keys of God's guidance. There are times in our Christian life when we are at the point of decision and it seems a thousand voices are clamoring at once to be heard. You may hear the voice of the Lord speaking to your heart, giving you specific direction for your life, but then in the midst of seeking confirmation and God's timing on the matter (two of the seven keys) other words that come from godly counsel or prophetic ministry (two more keys) can seem to cloud the issue. Suddenly you don't have peace (another key). What do you do?

The answer is to consider *all* of the keys, not just one or two.

One of the primary ways we can discern between the voice of God and any other voice is if we sense the peace of God in the midst of us. The voice that is accompanied with peace is usually the voice of God. The voice that is harried, hurried, and fearful, is either the voice of Satan, or it comes from our own human nature.

By this time, the apostle Paul had walked with the Lord for many years. He recognized the voice of God and was able to discern it from the other 3 voices. When the respected prophet Agabus declared the word of the Lord, Paul had to consider all the seven keys. In the end, Paul took the words of Agabus as confirmation of what the Lord was already speaking to his heart—he just differed in the interpretation of the word.

Paul continued on to Jerusalem and a few days later, he was seized in the temple. From this point forward in the book of Acts, Paul is a prisoner—but some of his most dramatic ministry came as a result of his obedience to the voice of the Lord, even facing danger and death. He spoke before Jewish leaders and Roman rulers, declaring boldly the gospel of grace. Finally, he stood before Caesar himself, the most powerful man in the world at that time.

So, did Agabus give a false word? I don't think so. Paul *was bound and delivered to the gentiles*, even though it was the Jewish religious leader's intention to kill him. The actions that the Jews took against Paul caused the Roman guard to send out his men to quell the riot. Though Agabus may have given his own interpretation of the vision that he saw, his word to Paul did come to pass. The apostle Paul was mature enough in his faith to receive and consider what the disciples and Agabus had declared, and to continue to follow the leading of the Holy Spirit.

God is speaking in all of these ways today to those in the Church who are listening.

Jesus Loves the Little Children

A friend recently told me her story of growing in faith to be able to listen to the direction of the Holy Spirit in her life. As a result of her obedience to the Spirit's direct guidance, orphan children half-way around the world were cared for in a very specific way.

> "No, you're wrong, Lord." Stephanie said aloud. "I've been to Kmart, Wal-Mart, Target, Academy, Sears, and Dillard's searching for boots."
>
> Stephanie Blackstone, the founder of the "Treasures of the Heart" ministry, provided aid to six orphanages in Russia. But nothing prepared her for what she saw at *Borskoe Gorodische.* She was shocked when she saw children in the cold Russian winter wearing worn out shoes—or no shoes at all. Now it was April and she could not shake the images of the children and their shoes from her mind.
>
> The 300-year-old building that housed the orphanage had once been a Russian Orthodox Church. A wide path next to the church wound down the slope to a picture perfect river. In spite of the beautiful scenery, the facilities

inside the orphanage were horrible. The building had been left in disrepair to a few adults who were committed to care for these abandoned children. It was cold and dilapidated, but it was the only home these children had. Alex, the director, made an agreement with the government that if they would pay his workers he would find a way to feed the children. These workers came faithfully every day even though they had not been paid for the last eight months.

They were living on the edge of survival when Stephanie arrived. Rugged conditions existed within the concrete walls. Live electrical wires dangled from wall sockets exposing children to more danger. The limited heat in deep winter didn't cut the bitter chill. Hand-me-downs were layered on for the only insulation for these weather-beaten children.

The kitchen was bare and the wooden floor had rotted and collapsed into the dirt below. The 99 youngsters needed more than walls and food. Their feet had outgrown the already worn-out shoes. The bitter cold of 20 degrees below zero was on the way.

Growing toes were peeking out of the holes in the well-worn shoes they were wearing. The deteriorated leather had broken in layers and was matted with manure fragments from the pastures where the children played among the milk cows. Stephanie knew those shoes wouldn't make it through a harsh winter.

How would they fare without proper shoes in the filth and ice? Stephanie wondered.

When she returned to Texas, Stephanie sought funds to buy the children shoes. Thinking of the harsh Russian weather, she decided to purchase boots that would last longer than regular shoes. The money donated, however, allowed only $12 for each child.

Stephanie suffers with severe idiopathic edema, which causes swelling. She usually reclines on Monday to recover after Sunday activities. This particular Monday she shrugged off the still small voice urging her to look for boots at the local Kmart.

No store in our warm climate has boots, certainly not in early spring. People seldom, if ever, needed winter boots in southeast Texas.

Still the spiritual messenger insisted, "Go to Kmart now."

"Ok, I'll go," she relented.

She entered Kmart and made her way straight to the shoe department, certain there would be no winter boots. A well-dressed gentleman approached her. "May I help you?" he asked deliberately, as if he knew he was supposed to appear at just this moment.

A little surprised, Stephanie chuckled. "Only if you have heavy-duty winter boots. I need 99 pairs in children's sizes!" she said, almost challenging him to respond.

Wondering what this distinguished-looking gentleman was doing in the K-Mart shoe department, she asked curiously, "Who are you?"

"I happen to be the buyer for the shoe department at this Kmart," he said with a smile. "What sizes do you need?" he asked.

Still joking Stephanie said flatly, "Every size."

"Funny thing," he said, his voice sounding puzzled, but intrigued. "I just received a shipment of boots that weren't ordered for this store, and I didn't know why."

Astonished, Stephanie allowed him to show her the "miraculous" merchandize. She then explained the situation to him. He went to work, sorting and stacking. He loaded box after box of boots onto a large shopping cart.

Many were already marked as sale merchandise. He marked the others half price. There were boots for boys, girls, and teenagers, a wide selection of sizes for kids, 7-17 years of age.

"I don't know how many pairs there are, but I hope these help," he said after he had the cart piled high with an assortment of boots.

Astounded by the surprise shopping spree, Stephanie replied, "I am amazed by this. Thank you for your kind generosity."

Her van was brimming with boots. She thanked God, in awe of how He had provided for the orphans in such a specific way. Stephanie offered up a prayer of gratitude that she had responded to the spiritual messenger.

The total bill averaged out to $12 a pair, and there were exactly 99 pairs of boots. Each child would have a pair for the winter!

These miracle boots were shipped in a cargo container to England in July, caravanned through Belgium, Germany, Poland, and Belarus before they were delivered on what was Russia's Christmas Day, just before the temperatures dipped to 20 degrees below freezing. And all because Stephanie listened to the voice she heard, stepped out of her comfort zone, and entered into the exciting adventure of life led by the Holy Spirit!

Changed into "Another Man"

A dramatic example of God's Spirit moving in the life of just a typical person is found in the story of Israel's first king, Saul. This physically-strong man was emotionally and spiritually weak. When the Lord revealed to the prophet

Samuel that Saul was to be king, Samuel relayed the message to the timid young man. Saul's response to the Old Testament prophet was:

> Saul replied, "Am I not a Benjamite, of the smallest of the tribes of Israel, and my family the least of all the families of the tribe of Benjamin? Why then do you speak to me in this way?"
> —1 Samuel 9:21, NASB

Samuel wasn't moved by his response, because the Lord had already made it plain that Saul would be the new king.

The next day Samuel took a flask of oil, poured it on Saul's head, kissed him and said:

> Has not the Lord anointed you a ruler over His inheritance?
> —1 Samuel 10:1, NASB

Then he began to foretell the events that would unfold during the coming day. After giving him many details of his coming journey, Samuel declared to Saul:

> Afterward you will come to the hill of God where the Philistine garrison is; and it shall be as soon as you have come there to the city, that you will meet a group of prophets coming down from the high place with harp, tambourine, flute, and a lyre before them, and they will be prophesying. *Then the Spirit of the Lord* will come upon you mightily, and *you shall prophesy* with them *and be changed into another man.*
> —1 Samuel 10:5-6, NASB

It all happened just as Samuel said. God changed Saul's heart and all those signs came about on that day. The Spirit of God came upon Saul mightily and he prophesied among the prophets. It came about, when all who knew him previously saw that he prophesied now with the prophets, that the people said to one another:

> ...What has happened to the son of Kish? *Is Saul also among the prophets?*
> —1 Samuel 10: 11, NASB, emphasis mine

When we yield to the Spirit of God, we are truly changed *into another man,* just a Saul was. We become the Kingdom Christians that God intends for us to be. We stop just seeing the Kingdom, and we begin to enter the Kingdom and participate in it. We're no longer just spectators in the stands, we're players on the field, following the direction of the coach, and scoring big points for the team.

In the foreword to Cindy Jacobs' book *The Voice of God,* Jack Hayford writes:

> That God *today* talks with His people is so basic to the Bible's promise and so abounding in the healthy and healing evidence of its fruit among believers, it should never be doubted or rejected. But it is. It is denied by those who fear that an uncontrolled access to, or an unpatrolled wall against such a warm, interactive relationship with God might surrender the subject of "divine revelation" to unlimited, hopelessly subjective definition. They fear, in short, that if anyone can say, "God told me," then anyone can usurp the role of God, either through intentional deception or innocent ignorance of His true Word.
>
> That is not an unjustified fear. The history of mankind is littered with the carcasses of multitudes who have fallen prey to such deception. From the time of the fall of man

until the most recent headlines describing the destruction of a band of cultists, either emotionally damaged or physically dead by reason of the influence of an erratic "voice," the danger of deceptive "revelations" has continued.

Still, the Lord Jesus Christ gave pointed instructions encouraging our expecting to know an ongoing personal communion with God. Even more than an "allowance" of this blessedness in intimacy and confidential communication between the Father and His redeemed children, Jesus promised it! And He gave the specific terms around which such interaction of a human with the Almighty may be founded. [23]

Those who accept my commandments and obey them are the ones who love me. And because they love me, my Father will love them. And I will love them and reveal myself to each of them.

—John 14:21, NLT

In my life I have seen some of the extremes that Pastor Hayford talks about. My parents came to Christ in the late 1960s and became a part of a charismatic community. As a child in a Christian school we did really "cool" things like witnessing in the park, marching in parades declaring "Jesus is Lord," and prophesying during chapel times. But I also experienced some of the "weirdness" of the time. There was an exclusivity that abounded—an attitude that said, "We have the truth and other churches aren't as mature or spiritually 'with it' as we are."

---

[23] Jacobs, Cindy, *The Voice of God,* Ventura, California: Regal Books, 1996, pp. 11-12.

As the 1970s progressed, the out-of-balance teachings of what became known as "the shepherding movement" began influencing the leaders of this community. Part of the manipulative aspect of the time included some "flaky" personal prophecy. There were some people who would speak "a word" to another telling them to do thus and thus, go here or there, marry this person or that—and there was not the mature spiritual oversight in place to give proper judgment and guidance regarding what was being "shared." As a result, some people made unwise decisions based on what became known as "parking lot prophecies" and suffered some serious consequences.

Sadly, as a result of these consequences, some people abandoned personal prophecy altogether. Others were so hurt that they suffered shipwreck in their spiritual lives and have yet to recover. This is a shame, because under proper guidelines and spiritual oversight, New Testament prophecy is a wonderful gift from the Lord (we will look at this in detail later).

Not all of this was done out of improper motives. Much of it happened out of sheer ignorance. Many of the leaders of this community were not much more mature in the Lord than the people they were supposed to be leading. Their understanding of proper biblical leadership was in its infancy. Many of these people had come out of mainstream churches where the Bible was looked upon merely as a collection of inspirational stories. Others had come out of the drug and hippie culture of the Jesus movement with little or no biblical knowledge at all.

On the other hand, there were some who were looking to control other people in order to stroke their own ego or build their own kingdom. There will always be wolves among the sheep. Unfortunately, some of them came to the party dressed like shepherds. Over time their true colors were revealed, but not before several people suffered from their spiritual abuse.

My parents, and others who lived through this time, learned to forgive and move on to find genuine, biblical leadership. I thank God for my Father, because he never let the wounds that he suffered in that season cause him to lose his faith in Christ or the Church. For him, it was never about the people around him, it was always about Jesus.

Dad always had a voracious appetite for the things of God. When it became apparent that the leaders of the community had become too controlling, my parents left and started searching for a new church home. After spending a few years at a Pentecostal Holiness church, and a few more at an Assembly of God church, we finally landed at an independent charismatic church that was strong in what was called the "word of faith movement." While there was a devotion to Scripture and freedom in the spirit at this church, there were not a strong set of guidelines for the proper flow of the spirit in the life of the individual Christian.

Then one day as the pastor was praying for guidance for the coming year, the Lord spoke clearly to him: "I am about to replace the foundations of this church. I am doing a new thing and establishing my pillars in this place."

Just a few months before this, one of the men in the church had given him Dr. Bill Hamon's book, *Prophets and Personal Prophecy*. He had not had a chance to read it, but after the New Year he picked it up and began thumbing through it. What he discovered in this book would revolutionize his life and the life of the church.

While there had been charismatic ministry in this local church, there was not a systematic structure to it. The pastor began teaching on the proper procedures for both giving and receiving personal prophecy. He taught on the different ways that we receive prophetic ministry in the church. We learned about prophetic terminology, the timing of God, the word, will, and way of God's guidance and much more. We learned to properly "test all things, and hold on to that which is good.

> Do not stifle the Holy Spirit. Do not scoff at prophecies, but test everything that is said. Hold on to what is good.
> —1 Thessalonians 5:19-22, NLT

The biblical principles I learned in that season have propelled my spiritual life forward and led me into ministry opportunities that have been nothing short of amazing. Sometimes God uses spectacular methods to reveal His will, such as personal prophecy, dreams, or visions. At other times it is a "still small voice" like the one that Elijah heard (see 1 Kings 19). No matter what method God chooses to unfold His will, the life lived following God is truly a great adventure.

God reveals Himself and His ways to those who are willing to press in to the things of His kingdom, by His spirit. That's why Jesus taught us to pray:

> Your kingdom come, your will be done, on earth as it is in heaven.
> —Matt 6:10, NASB

You could replace a few of those words to personalize it. "Your kingdom come, your will be done, in my life as it is in heaven." This kind of humble prayer moves the heart of God. He is looking for those who are willing to lay down their own agenda to be used by God to reach those who are lost. God's plan is to reconcile this fallen world to Himself (see 2 Corinthians. 5:18-19), and He is looking for those who would say, "Here I am, send me."

Jesus gave us this promise:

> Those who accept my commandments and obey them are the ones who love me. And because they love me, my Father will love them. And I will love them and reveal myself to each of them.
>
> —John 14:21, NLT

God reveals Himself and His ways to those who are surrendered to Him in every area of their lives. This doesn't mean being perfect—because that won't happen until Jesus returns—it means being willing to be willing, and quickly repenting when we fall into sin. It means following Jesus' example in the Garden of Gethsemane and declaring, "Not my will, but Yours be done" (Luke 22:42).

Walk in the Spirit and Not in the Flesh

In Romans 8, Paul exhorts disciples to walk in the Spirit and not in the flesh. Jesus is our example of being led by the Spirit. He prayed and then He did what the Father led Him to do. Then He taught us to do the same:

> Yes, I am the vine; you are the branches. Those who remain in me, and I in them, will produce much fruit. For apart from me you can do nothing.
>
> —John 15:5, NLT

Spending time in God's presence is key to knowing His will. In our pride we may think that we know what is best for our lives—even better than God sometimes. But when we come into His presence, He shows us our weakness and reveals His strength. He shows us our inadequacy and reveals His sufficiency. He shows us our need for direction and reveals His wisdom. If we approach the Lord with a heart to know and obey His will then we can trust that God will lead us in our decision making process.

Such was the case for Tama Westman, my friend who told me this story:

> I wondered if I was reaching anyone at all. A Christian writer with a column in a secular paper (Minnesota's *Chaska Herald*), I longed to live up to Matthew 5:16 and be a light to my world. I knew that sometimes believers are the only reflection of Christ the world sees, and my articles motivated, encouraged and expounded the virtues of our community. But was I *really* making a difference?
>
> One day my editor asked me to cover the story of a local teenager giving a talk on organ donation to his high school leadership training class. I was surprised when the boy's mother—a short, bubbly burst of energy—showed up a few minutes early, only to leave us before her son began his presentation. She hugged the shy teen and seemed proud of what he was about to do—but then she was gone. *I would have stayed*, I thought to myself. *What could be so important as to pull her away from her son's special moment?*

His ball cap pulled low to shade eyes that brimmed easily with tears, the 16-year- old walked fellow students through the day his father died of a brain aneurysm. And while his message promoted organ donation, the message *I* received was quite different: Call his mother. The words repeated in my head all day long. Finally obeying, the next morning I phoned her.

She told me the bank had called to offer condolences just two days after her husband's funeral and then asked when she would be out of her house.

"Excuse me?" she replied in amazement.

"Your house was sold in a sheriff's sale two months ago. Surely you knew?"

She had no idea. And now her family was in serious trouble. She couldn't stay to hear her son's speech—she had work to do.

After I hung up, God spoke again to my heart. He showed me that I could make a difference right here, right now, with this woman and her family. Reaching out through my writing would be a way for me to demonstrate God's love. I wrote one column about the son's presentation. Then I wrote a follow-up column—alerting the community to this family in need among us.

That column seized the heart of our town and my editor was inundated with phone calls: "How can I help?" "What do they need?" Food items and casseroles filled the freezers of neighbors up and down the family's block as people pitched in to feed a widow and four hungry boys. Then, due to the outpouring of our town's goodwill, the local Housing Authority went to bat for the family and reversed the sheriff's sale—an unheard of feat.

But the crisis was not over yet. They still needed nearly $20,000 in order to keep their home. Donations accumulated in a memorial fund set up at the bank, and in a matter of weeks, they had $32,000. *Thank you Chaska, You Saved My House* was the banner headline in that week's newspaper.

God showed me through this situation how my writing could impact my community for Christ—person by person, family by family. "Oh, that You would bless me indeed, and enlarge my territory," says the prayer of Jabez (1 Chronicles 4:10). God had blessed indeed and enlarged my territory. And although I was only its bearer—like a modern day Nineveh, our town was prepared for the message I delivered. Had I not obeyed the Father's call on *my* heart, I might have forestalled the blessings He bestowed on this family, my community and me. We all might have missed seeing Christ among us.[24]

God will lead us in love and fatherly concern, and He will go out of His way to keep us in His will if we follow His leading, like Tama did. If we approach the Lord with a heart to know and obey His will then we can trust that God will lead us in our decision making process. We can expect the Spirit of God to speak directly to our spirit. If we obey that leading, we will see amazing things take place in our lives—and in the lives that are touched through our act of obedience.

Now let's examine how the Holy Spirit also leads through visions, through dreams, and even through the desires He places in our hearts.

---

[24] Westman, Tama. Email to the author.

Questions For Meditation

1. Read Acts 13:1-4. How was the decision made to set apart Barnabas and Saul?

   Among the prophets and teachers of the church at Antioch of Syria were Barnabas, Simeon (called "the black man"), Lucius (from Cyrene), Manaen (the childhood companion of King Herod Antipas), and Saul. One day as these men were worshiping the Lord and fasting, the Holy Spirit said, "Appoint Barnabas and Saul for the special work to which I have called them." So after more fasting and prayer, the men laid their hands on them and sent them on their way.
   So Barnabas and Saul were sent out by the Holy Spirit. They went down to the seaport of Seleucia and then sailed for the island of Cyprus.
   —Acts 13:1-4, NLT

2. Read Hebrews 5:14. According to this verse, how do we learn to discern the voice of God in a situation?

   Solid food is for those who are mature, who through training have the skill to recognize the difference between right and wrong.
   —Hebrews 5:14, NLT

3. How have you heard the voice of the Spirit in your heart? Does God's voice sound different from your own inner voice?

4. Have you ever heard from the Lord, but added your own interpretation to what was said? What were the results? What did you learn from this experience?

5. Is there anyone that you need to forgive? Could the lack of forgiveness be hindering your prayers? Right now, write down a list of anyone that you need to forgive. Ask the Lord to give you the grace and strength to release them from their trespasses against you.

CHAPTER SIX

HEARING GOD'S VOICE THROUGH DESIRES, DREAMS & VISIONS

I am led by the Holy Spirit and this burning fire in my soul—for Africa.

—Reinhart Bonnke

Being Led Through the Desires of Your Heart

If you make the Lord first in your life, often He will place a burning desire or passion to do a certain thing into your heart that will become a driving force to accomplish His will, as He did for Reinhart Bonnke. This little known German evangelist started out witnessing on street corners, but he could not shake this passion to see souls won for Christ on the continent of Africa. Today, millions of people are Christians because this brave man refused to be stopped from seeing God's purposes fulfilled in his life.

Follow the fire of desire that God places within you. T. L. Osborne said:

> The desires that God has placed in you are vibrant proof that He destines your life for joy and great purpose. Believe it!"[25]

My father is a brilliant portrait painter. It doesn't matter where he goes, or what he's doing, he always finds a way to come back to his desire to do portraits. He once told me that if they took away his oils he would use acrylics; if they took away his acrylics he would use pastels; if they took his pastels he'd find a crayon; if they took that from him, he'd draw in the dirt with a stick. He explained to me that he didn't paint because that's what he did, he painted because that's who he is. God planted this desire in his heart and it has shaped his entire life.

The great revivalist preacher Charles Finney wrote concerning God's Guidance:

> If, then, you find yourself strongly drawn to desire a certain blessing, you are to understand it as an intimation that God is willing to bestow that particular blessing, and so you are bound to believe it. God does not trifle with His children. He does not put within them a desire for something to turn them off with something else. But He incites the very desires He is willing to gratify. And when

---

[25] Osborn, T.L. The Power of Positive Desire", Tulsa: Harrison House Publishers, 1996.

they feel such desires, people are bound to follow them through until they get the blessing.

When the Spirit of God is upon you and inspires strong desires for a particular blessing, you are bound to pray for it in faith. You are bound to infer from the fact that you find yourself drawn to desire such a thing that these desires are the work of the Spirit. Unless motivated by the Spirit of God, people are not apt to want the right kinds of things.[26]

By His Spirit, the Lord will use our sanctified desires to lead us into the fullness of His will for our lives! What do you think about day and night? What are you passionate about? What possibilities thrill your heart when you think or hear about them? These could well be the call of God on your life. Pay attention to your desires, and ask the Lord to confirm them through the other keys to His guidance.

Hearing God's Voice Through Dreams

For God speaks again and again, though people do not recognize it. He speaks in dreams, in visions of the night, when deep sleep falls on people as they lie in their beds. He whispers in their ears and terrifies them with warnings.
—Job 33:14-16, NLT

Through His Spirit, God speaks to people in dreams. The apostle Peter, speaking on the day of Pentecost in Acts chapter 2, quoted from the book of Joel declaring:

---

[26] Finney, Charles. *Revival Lectures*, "Lecture V: The Prayer of Faith."

> "In the last days," God says, "I will pour out my Spirit upon all people. Your sons and daughters will prophesy. Your young men will see visions, and your old men will dream dreams."
>
> —Acts 2:17, NLT

Joseph was one person in the Bible who had amazing dreams from the Lord, but when he shared them with his family they ridiculed him. Years later, after they had sold him into slavery, God delivered Joseph from prison and he became an interpreter of Pharaoh's dreams. Before he knew it he was in charge of all of Egypt under Pharaoh. After that his family wasn't laughing at him any more—they were bowing down before him, just as God had revealed in the dream.

There's a long history of God speaking to people in dreams. Nebuchadnezzar had a dream and brought it to Daniel. God gave Daniel the interpretation, laying out before the king all the things that the dream predicted. We are still seeing this dream unfold prophetically today!

According to John and Paula Sandford, one of the reasons God chooses to communicate to us through dreams is that in one fast-moving reel, God may speak with minimum conscious interference.[27] The Bible clearly links dreams, visions, and prophetic utterances. It's not uncommon for God to speak to His people through dreams. I keep a journal next to my bed so that if the Lord reveals something to me in a dream I can write is down immediately when I wake. Sadly,

---

[27] Sandford, John & Paula, *The Elijah Task*, Tulsa, OK: Victory House, 1977, p. 170.

many people wait to write their dreams and they often forget some or many of the important details—or even forget about the dream altogether. Others ignore their dreams, thinking they are merely an unimportant part of their subconscious.

Dreams from the Lord can be:

- Warnings of danger;

- Proclamation of events or announcements;

- Used to give direction;

- Used to give comfort;

- Used by God to bring emotional healing; or

- Used by God to call His people into intercession and action.

If you believe you have received a dream from the Lord, but are unsure what it means, ask the Holy Spirit to give you the interpretation of what God is trying to say to you. It's also good to share the dream with a trusted pastor, mentor, or parent. But don't just share it with anyone. Some people cannot keep a confidence, and others are not spiritually mature enough to have insight into what God is saying. Ask the Lord to guide you to the right people to talk to about your dream.

If the dream remains a mystery, but you sense it is from the Lord, don't be too hasty to throw it away. It may be that the interpretation will come in time. Some dreams, like some prophecies, take years to come to pass or to understand.

Cindy Jacobs warns:

If the dream seems to indicate a change in life's direction, seek guidance from those in spiritual authority to confirm what you believe God is saying to you. The dream may be for someone else. Ask the Lord if and/or when you should share it with the person. It may be something you need to pray about yourself, thus allowing the Lord to avert the situation without worrying the other person.[28]

Like all the other ways the Lord will direct us, a dream should be tested against the other keys of God's guidance. If it is of the Lord it will line up with Scripture and you will have an enduring peace that the Spirit is leading your through it.

You may be disturbed by the dream at first, and that uncomfortable feeling may linger. But if it is from the Lord, He will give you an assurance that He is speaking to you, even if it is unsettling for a time.

Dreams can be a part of God's guidance, but be cautious; many dreams have no meaning whatsoever. They are merely a function of our brain on auto-pilot while we sleep. Dreams can come from the subconscious, or they can be brought on by indigestion, emotional pressures, or anxiety. Like all other potential direction, test any dream against the seven keys of God's guidance, and hold on to that which is good.

Hearing God's Voice Through Visions

A vision is direct communication from God where He illuminates His purposes in such a clear way that they are unmistakable. A vision can be open—so real that the person

---

[28] Jacobs, Cindy, *The Voice of God,* Ventura, California: Regal Books, 1996, p. 217.

senses that what he or she is seeing is actually happening right in front of them. Or a vision can be in our mind's eye, or as some would say, our sanctified imagination. John and Paula Sandford describe visions as "the picture language of God."[29] The important difference between dreams and visions is that when we receive a vision we are awake, so visions are much more subject to our control.

The Lord used a vision to break Peter away from his traditional religious moorings at the house of Cornelius (see Acts 10). As a result of this encounter the Gospel was preached to the Gentiles and they were born again and baptized in the Holy Spirit. Later, when some of the more legalistic believers in Jerusalem questioned why Peter would do this, he told them the vision and how it was confirmed through Cornelius. He also recounted how the Holy Spirit came upon the Gentiles as He had come upon the Jews on the day of Pentecost. The dramatic way that the Lord confirmed the vision silenced the critics and the Good News was proclaimed to the rest of the world.

It's interesting to note in this scenario that Cornelius "saw clearly in a vision an angel of God coming in" and calling his name (Acts 10:3). Though he was a God-fearing man, Cornelius was not yet a disciple of Jesus Christ. God has often used visions to capture the attention of non-believers to bring them to salvation. In fact, we have numerous reports in our own time of Jesus appearing to people in countries that are closed to the Gospel, revealing Himself as God

---

[29] Sandford, John and Paula. *The Elijah Task*, Tulsa: Victory House, 1977, 170.

through visions and dreams, and as a result they have received Him as their Savior!

One of the most powerful incidences of supernatural guidance is the story of Saul on the road to Damascus. In this scenario Saul has an open vision of a tremendous light, he hears an audible voice (though his companions heard the voice, but saw no one). Then in Damascus, the Lord also appeared to Ananias in a vision telling him to go and pray that Saul's sight be restored. Ananias obeyed God and prophesied to Saul that He would be an Apostle to the Gentiles.

Why did God resort to such a dramatic form of guidance with Saul? For one, Jesus told Saul,

> Saul, Saul, why do you persecute me? It is hard for you to kick against the goads.
> —Acts 26:14, NIV

The King James says, "It is hard for thee to kick against the pricks." I believe the Holy Spirit had been working on Saul's heart for some time—perhaps since the stoning of Stephen who gave such a tremendous witness for the Lord. The spirit of conviction must have been burning in his heart. But Saul was a zealous Pharisee who thought he was diligently serving God by harassing the Christians. It would take a dramatic event to get his attention—and God sovereignly did just that.

The other reason God may have resorted to such an unusual display of His power and glory was to set a marker in Saul's life that he would not forget when he was faced with persecution later in his ministry. The Lord ordained great things for the ministry of Saul, who would become Paul, but he also warned of great suffering and persecution. In his vision, God told Ananias,

But the Lord said to Ananias,

> Go! This man is my chosen instrument to proclaim my name to the Gentiles and their kings and to the people of Israel. I will show him how much he must suffer for my name's sake.
>
> —Acts 9:15-16 NIV

The Bible tells us that Paul had a dynamic ministry, establishing churches, traveling around the world, preaching before kings, casting out demons, healing the sick, and leading many to the Lord. But we also see the persecution that he suffered for the sake of the Gospel:

> Five times I received at the hands of the Jews the forty lashes less one. Three times I was beaten with rods. Once I was stoned. Three times I was shipwrecked; a night and a day I was adrift at sea; on frequent journeys, in danger from rivers, danger from robbers, danger from my own people, danger from Gentiles, danger in the city, danger in the wilderness, danger at sea, danger from false brothers; in toil and hardship, through many a sleepless night, in hunger and thirst, often without food, in cold and exposure. And, apart from other things, there is the daily pressure on me of my anxiety for all the churches.
>
> —2 Cor. 11:24-28, ESV

I have met people who have said, "How I would love to have an open vision, or see an angel, or hear the audible voice of God." But they neglect to take into account that the Lord will often require much, in both service and suffering, from those to whom He reveals Himself in such a dynamic way. The Lord spoke to Saul in direct proportion to the challenges and persecution he would face as the apostle Paul. I believe He needed such a dynamic display to sustain him and keep him moving forward in Christ amidst the great difficulties that confronted him. Thank God that Paul didn't back down from this daunting assignment. In his defense before King Agrippa he referred back to this amazing encounter with the Lord Jesus Christ:

> ...I obeyed that vision from heaven. I preached first to those in Damascus, then in Jerusalem and throughout all Judea, and also to the Gentiles, that all must repent of their sins and turn to God — and prove they have changed by the good things they do.
>
> —Acts 26:19-20, NLT

In the midst of the trials and persecution, Paul was able to persevere and overcome, in part because of this tremendous revelation from God.

God speaks in visions. God speaks in dreams. God speaks in a still, small voice. He speaks from the Bible, and he speaks from circumstances—and it is all by His Spirit to your spirit.

Discerning the Voice of God

If we are saved, the Holy Spirit dwells within us, guiding us into God's truth for our lives. In order to live the victorious life God intends for us, we must train ourselves to hear and respond to this leading of the Spirit. We do this by first recognizing it is God speaking, and then by acting on His direction.

It's so important to continue to grow in Christ and in the knowledge of God's Word. Like the Children of Israel wandering in the dessert, we can't live on yesterday's manna—we must have the fresh bread of heaven for today to remain strong in the Lord.

Examine yourself. Are you teachable? Are you seeking to learn more? Or do you feel that what you have learned about God and His ways is sufficient. Attending Christian school, Sunday school, Bible College, cell groups, Sunday morning services, conferences, and seminars are all important. But these things comprise merely the foundation, not the end of our learning experiences. Like Peter praying on the rooftop at lunch time, we must make time to commune with God on a daily basis throughout our lives in order to truly discern His voice. As we act on that leading and see God move in our lives, we will grow in confidence that we are truly hearing His voice. Then as we prove ourselves faithful in obedience to His leading, God will increase His revelation in our lives.

Hearing God Through Times of Prayer

Prayer is communion with God—it is talking to Him and then listening for Him to talk to you. It is the closest, most intimate relationship with the Creator you can have on this earth. "Deep calls unto deep," the Bible says in Psalm 42:7. In prayer, the depths of your spirit are in communion with the depths of the Spirit of God. Out of this you can begin to discern the heart of God as He gives you instruction, guidance, or a burden to pray for certain things.

Believers should build into their schedules daily quiet time alone with God in prayer and Bible study. But in addition to this, Christians should always be in an attitude of communion with God, ready to pray at any moment.

Prayer can take place in any circumstance. Throughout the day, as events pass by, I may find myself talking to the Lord, asking for advice and counsel, or for favor and blessing. Sometimes I just worship God and tell Him I love Him with no other agenda—some call this "soaking" or "meditational" prayer. The Christian's life should be filled with prayer.

We must remember that prayer is rooted in forgiveness. Jesus taught in the Lord's Prayer that we are to pray,

> ... and forgive us our sins, as we have forgiven those who sin against us.
>
> —Matthew 6:12, NLT

The relationship of God's people to Him comes about because of continuous forgiveness—He forgives us, and we forgive others.

If we are going to hear God's voice, and see miracles in our lives, we have to be willing to forgive other people, even as God is willing to forgive us. In fact, Jesus said that unless we forgive, God will not hear our prayers at all—and that is a sobering thought.

Be Careful of False Guidance

It's clear that people everywhere want to hear from God. You only have to do a web search for "astrology," "fortune-telling," "séances," and so forth to see how hungry people are for God's voice. But these things are merely cheap and dangerous counterfeits of how God wants to communicate with people. The Bible makes it clear that God will only communicate with man through the Holy Spirit, and not through some astrologer, soothsayer, or medium. In fact, to seek guidance through such means is an abomination to the Lord and will bring a curse in your life (see Deuteronomy 18:9-14; Leviticus 19:31; Is. 8:11 & 19; Is. 2:6; and Micah 5:12).

The consequences for seeking guidance outside the biblical pattern are severe—they could even affect your eternal salvation. There is a difference between hearing God's voice in a biblical manner by the Holy Spirit, and seeking God through New Age false prophets. It's easy to be deceived. That's why we need to know the Word of God and use it as our guide to truth in this life. Stay within the biblical guidelines of the seven keys and you will walk in both safety and the blessing of God.

Rejoicing in Relationship

You should not feel inferior when you hear stories of supernatural guidance or revelation from the Lord to other Christians if you yourself have not had these types of experiences. God leads us as individuals. He will speak to us and lead our footsteps in the way He chooses. I have never heard the audible voice of God. There are other spiritual experiences others have had that are biblical, and I'd actually like to experience some day, but God has not chosen to speak in those ways in my life up to this time. We need to remember, it's not about the supernatural experience, it's about our relationship with Him.

When Jesus sent out the 70 disciples in His name, they returned with excitement about their ability to cast out demons and heal the sick. Jesus responded:

> ...I have given you authority over all the power of the enemy, and you can walk among snakes and scorpions and crush them. Nothing will injure you. But don't rejoice because evil spirits obey you; *rejoice because your names are registered in heaven.*
> —Luke 10:19-20, NLT, emphasis mine

Even though God may not yet have chosen to lead us in some of these ways, we should always remain open to the possibility of His directing us supernaturally. We should also guard against having a cynical response to reports of supernatural guidance or events in the life of another believer. Our carnal reaction is often to assume that these reports are merely an allusion, or an exaggeration on the part of the person reporting it. The Bible makes it clear that God will guide His people supernaturally, and we should extend our faith to believe for such guidance in our lives. That's what it means to walk in the spirit, and to enter the kingdom of God.

Dr. James Dobson rightly warns, however, that determining the will of God exclusively by the means of feelings or impressions can lead you away from God's plan for your life. He experienced what he called a "phony impression" on the day he completed his Ph.D. studies at the University of Southern California:

I had the prize I sought so diligently. Driving home that day, I expressed my appreciation to God for His obvious blessing on my life, and I asked Him to use me in any way He chose. The presence of the Lord seemed very near at that moment.

Then, as I turned a corner, I was seized by a strong impression that conveyed this unmistakable message: You are going to lose someone very close to you within the next 12 months. A member of your immediate family will die, but when it happens, don't be dismayed. Just continue trusting and depending on me.

I had not been thinking about death and was greatly alarmed by the threatening thought. My heart thumped a little harder as I contemplated who might die. When I reached my home, I told no one about the experience.

One month passed without a tragedy. Two and three months sped by and still death failed to visit my family. Finally, the anniversary of my morbid impression came and went without consequence. The impression had been invalid.

Through my counseling experiences, I have learned that my phony impression was not unique. Similar experiences are common, particularly among those who have not adjusted well to the challenge of living.[30]

We can hear God's voice, and as Christians we are led by the Spirit. But we must be careful when interpreting our feelings and these kinds of impressions. This is why the leading of the Spirit in our own heart is only one of the seven keys to hearing God. What we sense in our spirit must be weighed against the other keys.

---

[30] Dobson, James. *Complete Marriage and Family Home Reference Guide,* Carol Stream, IL: Tyndale, 2000.

Here's a helpful checklist to consider when weighing an impression against the other keys:

- Does the impression in your heart line up with Scripture? If you're not sure, do a thorough Bible study on the topic. You may want to get further advice from your spouse, pastor, or other mature Christians.

- Does the impression line up with other things you believe the Lord has spoken to your heart? In this you must be careful, especially when you are a younger Christian. Sometimes it's difficult to discern if what we are sensing is of the Lord, of the Devil, of our own fleshly desires, or a message that we have picked up from the world. In the multitude of counselors there is safety.

- Does the leading line up with any insight that you have received through a personal prophecy? Remember the admonition of the Apostle Paul:

    > Do not quench the Spirit. Do not despise prophecies. Test all things; hold fast what is good.
    > —1 Thessalonians 5:19-21

- Has the Lord confirmed the impression you have received through the mouth of two or three witnesses? These impressions must be confirmed outside of your own feelings or thoughts. God is willing and able to confirm what He has spoken to you in a number of ways. The more important the decision, the more vital for you to seek confirmation.

- Do you have peace about this leading? You may have assurance about one aspect of the counsel, but not all of it. Or, you may not have a peace about it at all. Wait until you have peace about your decision before moving forward.

- Does the impression jive with the circumstances of your life? It may be a great idea. It may line up with the Bible, with what God has said to you in the past, with prophetic words that you have received, with what other godly leaders have said to you, and with the peace in your heart. But if the circumstances are not lining up it may be that the timing to move forward on this direction is not right, or that it is just not God's will for your life. God gave us an intellect to help us determine what is the right thing to do. Part of the process of seeking God's will for your life includes asking yourself, "Does this make sense?" God won't have you do something that is foolish.

As you look forward, are you viewing the future with fear—or with faith? As believers, we must move forward with confidence, based on the eternal truth of God's Word. Take your cue from Joshua. After 40 years in the wilderness, the Israelites were finally poised to enter the Promised Land when Moses died. God tells Joshua,

> You must lead My people across the Jordan River into the land I am giving them ... Everywhere you go, you will be on land I have given you ... For I will be with you ... I will not fail you or abandon you.
>
> —Joshua 1:2b, 3b, 5b, NLT

God had promised His people a land flowing with milk and honey, filled with vineyards they didn't plant and cities they didn't build. It was theirs for the taking. But first they would have to fight!

God fortified Joshua for battle by exhorting him three times, *Be strong and courageous* (Joshua 1:6, 7, 9). In faith, Joshua led the Israelites across the Jordan to a miraculous triumph over Jericho—and then to victory after victory throughout the land! This was only possible because Joshua and his warriors sought the Lord's direction, and then took God at His word.

Today, God is still speaking to His people, declaring, *I will be with you! Be strong and courageous!* As He leads you by His Spirit move forward with boldness knowing that God is on your side and directing your steps.

Questions For Meditation

1. Read Job 33:14-16. What does this passage have to say about God's speaking through dreams?

    For God speaks again and again, though people do not recognize it. He speaks in dreams, in visions of the night, when deep sleep falls on people as they lie in their beds. He whispers in their ears and terrifies them with warnings.
    —Job 33:14-16, NLT

2. Has God ever spoken to you through a dream? What was the result of His leading in this way?

3. Read Deuteronomy 18:9-14; Leviticus 19:31; Isaiah 8:11 & 19; Isaiah 2:6; and Micah 5:12. What do these

scriptures say about consulting with mediums or astrologers? How strong are the warnings?

When you enter the land the Lord your God is giving you, be very careful not to imitate the detestable customs of the nations living there. For example, never sacrifice your son or daughter as a burnt offering. And do not let your people practice fortune-telling, or use sorcery, or interpret omens, or engage in witchcraft, or cast spells, or function as mediums or psychics, or call forth the spirits of the dead. Anyone who does these things is detestable to the Lord. It is because the other nations have done these detestable things that the Lord your God will drive them out ahead of you. But you must be blameless before the Lord your God. The nations you are about to displace consult sorcerers and fortune-tellers, but the Lord your God forbids you to do such things.
—Deuteronomy 18:9-14, NLT

Do not defile yourselves by turning to mediums or to those who consult the spirits of the dead. I am the Lord your God.
—Leviticus 19:31, NLT

The Lord has given me a strong warning not to think like everyone else does... Someone may say to you, "Let's ask the mediums and those who consult the spirits of the dead. With their whisperings and mutterings, they will tell us what to do." But shouldn't people ask God for guidance? Should the living seek guidance from the dead?
—Isaiah 8:11, 19, NLT

For the Lord has rejected his people, the descendants of Jacob, because they have filled their land with practices

from the East and with sorcerers, as the Philistines do. They have made alliances with pagans.
—Isaiah 2:6, NLT

I will put an end to all witchcraft, and there will be no more fortune-tellers.
—Micah 5:12, NLT

4. Why is it dangerous to be led by our feelings alone?

5. List some of the ways that people seek guidance outside of the biblical pattern. Then list corresponding Scripture verses that warn against such practices.

Chapter Seven

Godly Counsel - The Wisdom and Experience of Others

Plans succeed through good counsel; don't go to war without wise advice.

—Proverbs 20:18, NLT

It shouldn't have happened.

"Bob Slosser's writing class is the most popular one we have," the faculty secretary told me. "He sets a limit of 20 on the class, and there is always a waiting list of our communication students. Since you're a student in the Divinity School it's doubtful that there will be an opening. But if you like we can put you on the list..."

She didn't hold out much hope, but I insisted that I be placed on that precious list. I had been an admirer of Bob

Slosser for many years. Bob was a former *New York Times* editor, a published author, and the retired president of Regent University. I've always had a passion for writing, and I hold in high esteem those who meld their craft with their ministry; people like Jamie Buckingham, Ken Gire, Max Lucado, and Bob Slosser.

I attended Regent as a student in the Divinity School, but I hoped to take elective writing classes in the College of Communication. A friend told me I should take Bob Slosser's class, *The Craft of Good Writing*—that is, if I could get in.

A week later the faculty secretary called. "I can't explain it," she told me. "Only fifteen students have signed up for this class. I guess you're in."

I discovered later that a class required for graduation was scheduled at the same time as Bob's course. All the second year communication students who wanted to graduate were forced to forego *The Craft of Good Writing*. By God's grace I received my first opportunity to get to know this godly man.

Throughout the semester Bob encouraged us to look at writing as a ministry. "Make your words white-hot, hard-hitting, passionate," he declared.

The class was tough—brutal at times. Bob didn't pull any punches with his students. Like many aspiring writers I had romantic notions concerning the life of a wordsmith. Without apology he smashed those naïve assumptions to pieces. "Writing is painful," he declared, his face wrenched to mirror the statement. "It is just plain hard work. If you are to be a good writer, you will have to toil for countless hours to hone the craft."

For me it was sweet agony. Bob was painfully honest. But it made me better. It made me think. It made me stretch. It made me grow. I was sitting at the feet of a master writer—I knew I may never have this opportunity again. I wanted to make the most of it.

As the semester commenced, Bob's words about making writing a ministry burned in my soul. One day I learned of a new degree called religious journalism, which was designed for students who wanted to integrate writing with ministry. The degree required a year in the Divinity School and a-year-and-a-half in the Journalism School. I prayed about making the move and decided to seek godly counsel, so I set up a meeting with Dr. Slosser.

Although he didn't say "thus saith the Lord" to me in his reply, I knew he was prophesying as he spoke. His words shot through me like a laser beam: "There are a lot of 'right-thinking' pastors, Bible teachers, and missionaries out there, Craig. But there are not a lot of 'right-thinking' writers and communicators. If you believe this is what the Lord is saying to you, I am in absolute agreement."

I transferred into the Journalism program the next day and never looked back. From there the Lord has opened tremendous doors for me to minister through the media. I will always be appreciative to Bob as a teacher, mentor, and friend. His godly counsel helped to set the course for the rest of my life.

The writer of Proverbs declares:

> Plans go wrong for lack of advice; many advisers bring success.
>
> —Proverbs 15:22, NLT

Read the Book!

When I was in high school my father gave me advice I will never forget. "Read books and learn from them. All of the achievements and mistakes a person makes in a lifetime may be learned by reading their one book."

Seeking godly counsel is like reading a portion of someone's life story.

No one is an island to themselves in the Body of Christ. We all need to listen to the wisdom and experience of godly men and women who have walked farther with the Lord in life. There are a number of people who would qualify to give us godly counsel; our parents, a spouse, a pastor, a cell group leader, a professional Christian counselor, a youth group leader, a Sunday school teacher, another mature leader in a church, or a trusted and mature Christian friend.

In seeking godly counsel it's important that we maintain an attitude of humility. One of my former pastors used the metaphor of a ladder.

> You may be on the fifth rung in your life, and this man or woman of God is twenty rungs up above you. They have felt and experienced those twenty rungs, and they can give you advice based on that valuable experience.[31]

The apostle Peter gives us an excellent blueprint for how relationships are supposed to work between spiritual leaders and their followers. He speaks first to the elders:

> The elders who are among you I exhort ... shepherd the flock of God which is among you, serving as overseers, not

---

[31] Albanes, Rev. Larry. Sermon, First Assembly of God, Erie, PA.

by compulsion but willingly, not for dishonest gain but eagerly; nor as being lords over those entrusted to you, but being examples to the flock...

Then he addresses the younger disciples:

> Likewise you younger people, submit yourselves to your elders. Yes, all of you be submissive to one another, and be clothed with humility, for "God resists the proud, but gives grace to the humble." Therefore humble yourselves under the mighty hand of God, that He may exalt you in due time...
>
> —1 Peter 5:1-6, NKJV

The term "shepherd" that is used here is the metaphor that Jesus chose when he restored Peter to his apostleship after he had betrayed him. This word must have been burned into Peter's psyche, because Jesus used the concept three times after asking him is he loved him—once for every time that Peter denied knowing Christ. "Feed my sheep" Jesus said. Peter later passes the command on to the elders of the Church.

The Apostle Paul spoke of the need for spiritual fathers and mothers when he wrote:

> For though you have countless guides in Christ, you do not have many fathers.
>
> —1 Corinthians 4:15, ESV

There is a difference in relationship between an instructor and a father. A father can be an instructor, but an instructor is not a father. A father cares deeply for the overall well-being of the spiritual child, not just that he or she has learned the lesson.

This is the kind of person that a Christian should seek when looking for godly counsel.

The New Testament is filled with exhortations to respect authority, submit to godly leadership, and maintain discipline in the church and in our individual lives. We need to be accountable to some kind of godly leadership.

Considering Godly Counsel

In seeking this accountability, you want to align yourself with those who demonstrate humility, walking closely with the Lord. Look for a leader who lives out what he or she preaches. Are they guiding their own lives according to the Scriptures? This should be someone who prays publicly in church services, but also encourages people to have a strong private life of prayer and devotion.

You should feel confident and peaceful that this person truly cares about you. They should have your best interest at heart. They should continually encourage your relationship with the Lord through practical disciplines like reading your Bible and praying every day, staying in fellowship with other believers, and walking in holiness. This person should want the best for you for the sake of the Kingdom of God, for the church, and for you as an individual.

Biblical Examples

Throughout the Bible we see many examples of people who sought the wisdom of godly men and women when facing important decisions. A key story from the Old Testament was when Moses received input from his father-in-law, Jethro to organize the tribes of Israel and delegate responsibility and authority to trusted leaders (Exodus 18:13—27). Moses had been doing too much and spreading himself too thin. He wisely listened to Jethro's counsel to reorganize the tribes and delegate responsibility to other leaders. By doing so his work load was lightened, the nation of Israel was blessed, and the leaders who were chosen were released to do the things that God had called and equipped them to do.

Another interesting example of godly counsel is seen in the story of Paul choosing Timothy as one of his traveling companions (Acts 16:1–5). It's interesting to see that nothing is said in this passage of a dramatic revelation from God concerning Paul's choice of Timothy. There was no vision that we know of. There was no dream or prophetic utterance. Paul seems to follow the same advice he gave to other churches for choosing leadership. In his letters, Paul encouraged the church to make sound, practical choices, carefully examining the candidate's gifts, personality, and qualifications for the role.

In Acts 16, Timothy is described as *well-spoken of by the brethren* (verse 2). From this phrase we can deduce that Paul sought the advice of others as he considered Timothy's qualifications. He was told of Timothy's godly heritage. His father was also a Greek, a quality that might come in handy in Paul's ministry to the Gentiles. Luke also tells us that Timothy was a disciple—which means "disciplined follower"—so he was completely surrendered to the will of God.

After Paul considered all these things, he came to the determination that Timothy would be right for the job. This decision proved to be a good one. Later, Timothy would become a great leader in the early Church, and his personal ministry to Paul would last until the great apostle's final days.

Checks and Balances

When we receive godly counsel, we must always test it against the other six keys. Blaine Smith tells the story of the famous missionary William Carey who sensed an overwhelming call from God to the mission field. When he shared it with trusted leaders around him one man chastised him saying, "If God wants to save the heathen He can do it without your help." Although this man was a Christian, and the others who discouraged him from going were also believers, Carey ignored their counsel. William Carey knew God had called him to the mission field. He knew it both in what God had spoken to his heart and through confirmation of the Scriptures. He obeyed God's direction and the missionary movement of the Nineteenth Century was birthed. Today, many of the countries that received missionaries through Carey's efforts are now sending missionaries to other parts of the world.[32]

Sometimes when the people we trust as counselors have a check in their spirit about the guidance we are sensing it is an indication to wait until the Lord has made His will clear to us. We may sense that God is saying go one way, while our parents or pastors are sensing that it should be another way. In the end we may find that neither way was God's plan, and that there was a third alternative that we were to follow. By waiting we allow God to reveal His perfect will to us at the

---

[32] Smith, Blaine, *Guidance By the Book*, Virginia Beach, VA, CBN Publishing, 1992.

right time. And God is honored by our willingness to trust Him and humble ourselves while waiting for Him to open the right door.

Mistakes of the Past

Disappointments in guidance do happen, especially when people step out erroneously, basing their decision on a vision, dream, or prophecy without receiving the input of mature leaders. Other people reject godly counsel altogether, saying, "I can hear God perfectly well by myself." They willingly walk away from the safety that is only found in the multitude of counselors. This is dangerous ground. It's easy to fall into self-deception.

Because we are emotional beings, our feelings can sometimes interfere with our reason. God gave us a mind to help us to make rational decisions. Sometimes we want something so badly that we ignore God's leading and that which makes logical sense just to fulfill our fleshly desires. At other times we are so emotionally involved in a situation that we can't come to a rational decision. One day our heart is saying one thing, and the next day it's saying something else. At these times we need the help of others to sort through our feelings to find God's plan.

Another word of admonition: Don't seek counsel from someone who is in the middle of similar struggle. For example, a person who has been hurt by people in the church probably can't give you good counsel on finding a church of your own, at least until they have resolved their own issues. Try to find someone who will give you an objective opinion, not clouded by emotion.

The Sticky Issue of "Spiritual Abuse"

A final warning in the area of counsel is to be on guard for manipulative leaders. Be careful to avoid the pastor or spiritual leader who is caught up in what is called spiritual abuse. While the Bible makes it clear that we are to properly submit ourselves to leadership in the church, dictatorial leadership is never condoned by this command. Only Jesus Christ is Lord over our lives. No man or woman should assume that role.

There is clearly a biblical call for proper spiritual authority in the church, in the community and in the life of a believer. We need the input of other mature Christians in our lives. We need to seek the counsel of these wise disciples, especially in major decision. But as believers we have access to God's throne through a personal relationship with Jesus Christ. There is no need for a priest or minister to take the place of Jesus as Lord over our lives. We look to Him for guidance in our decisions, and then we seek confirmation and clarity from other brothers and sisters on what we sense the Lord is saying—we don't seek their permission.

Spiritual abuse can be difficult to detect if you have never encountered it. In a manipulative church, the pastor or senior leaders will position themselves in a way that takes the place of the Holy Spirit in people's lives. They will try to put undue influence on the choices of people in their congregation in order to coerce them to follow their lead. They might try to sway someone's decision in a matter to keep them under their control, or to keep them from leaving the church. People in a controlling church are often told they cannot leave the church with God's blessing unless the pastor approves the decision. They are warned that if they don't follow the pastor's guidance, not only will God not bless them, but they will also bring a curse upon themselves or their family. Leaving the "covering" of the church and the controlling pastor will result in some sort of calamity.

When a pastor tells his congregation that those who leave his church or disobey his authority are in danger of God's wrath, you can be sure this man or woman is operating in a spirit of control. He is attempting to sow fear as a carnal means of keeping people in his church.

Fear is the motivation behind such comments—not love. You can be sure this type of reasoning is not from God. Jesus never motivated people out of fear. Fear is a form of manipulation. Manipulation is sin.

The apostle John is called *the apostle of love* because he wrote so much about our call as Christians to walk in love.

> Such love has no fear, because perfect love expels all fear...
> —1 John 4:18, NLT

The minister who uses fear to manipulate is not walking in love; he or she is walking in control.

By keeping people in fear, controlling spiritual leaders strive to convince good Christian people to build *the leader's* religious kingdom—by telling them they are building the Kingdom of God. These controlling leaders are focused on their own needs being met, while the needs of the people are ignored.

Jesus was more critical of the manipulative religious leaders of His day than He was of the sinners, and for good reason. The scribes and Pharisees of that time put false religious burdens on the people for the sake of their own power and prosperity. In this case, as it is in controlling churches today, the people were burdened with rules and regulations that needed to be performed to gain the acceptance of these religious leaders. Many Christians today find themselves bearing the heavy load of the religious baggage in an abusive system. Around the world, hurting churchgoers struggle to earn the favor and approval of a modern-day Pharisee, all the while erroneously thinking they are seeking the favor of God.

If you are in Christ you already have God's favor. No amount of work for a spiritually abusive pastor will give you more acceptance than you already have.

Jesus recognized the burden being placed on sincere believers in His time, who just wanted to do what is right.

> They were bewildered (harassed and distressed and dejected and helpless), like sheep without a shepherd.
> —Matthew 9:36 AMPC

In his book, *Warning Signs of Spiritual Abuse*, Mike Fehlauer writes:

> A shepherd doesn't drive his sheep as cattlemen drive their cattle. A shepherd leads his sheep to a safe place where food is plentiful and where they can find rest.[33]

The Christian seeking guidance from a spiritual leader must also be on the lookout for the dangerous trap of spiritual elitism that can produce an "us and them," or a "fortress" mentality. This is a telltale sign of spiritual abuse.

---

[33] Fehlauer, Mike, Exposing Spiritual Abuse (Lake Mary, FL. Charisma House, 2001).

A church or pastor with an elitist attitude teaches, if ever so subtly, that no other church or ministry is preaching the pure gospel. An elitist leader will discourage members from visiting other churches or receiving counsel from anyone who doesn't attend their church. If anyone breaks this rule, he or she is viewed as rebellious.

A healthy spiritual leader, on the other hand, respects and encourages the other churches and ministries in a community, recognizing there are several different expressions of the Body of Christ. A spiritually free pastor realizes that no one denomination or local church can represent the love of Jesus to a city. A healthy church will promote revival in the entire Christian community. It will reject the idea that it has some kind of doctrinal or spiritual superiority.

In a healthy relationship, a spiritual mentor will provide godly counsel from selfless motives. He or she will want God's will for your life. If God ever calls you to leave the church or ministry, then they will rejoice that you are being sent out to be a blessing in another place.

Remember, godly counsel is only one of the seven keys of God's guidance. You should never rely solely on the advice or input from another human being in determining God's will for your life—regardless of how long they have been walking with the Lord.

There must be a balance between humbly seeking guidance from a person of spiritual authority, and subjecting yourself to the manipulative practice of spiritual abuse. Finding that balance is an ongoing process in life. But it is a necessary struggle that will prevent you from becoming weary and worn on one hand, trying to jump through religious hoops that promise God's acceptance and love—and on the other hand from becoming an island unto yourself, determining what is right in your eyes alone. Both sides of this spiritual spectrum are dangerous, and should be avoided.

Ask God to give you the grace and guidance to walk in the tension of these truths—opening yourself to the input of mature Christian leaders, while avoiding spiritual control. If you find yourself striving to gain the acceptance of spiritual leaders, or if your church constantly requires more and more of your life with no end in sight—and little encouragement or understanding of your needs along the way—then you may want to re-examine the church you are attending.

What Can I Do About It?

The more you walk with the Lord, and the more you act on God's leading and then see Him bless your obedience, the less you will need to rely on the input of others. This is what the New Covenant is all about, God's Spirit residing in you.

The Bible is clear on the issue:

> For there is one God, and there is one mediator between God and man, the man Christ Jesus.
> —1 Timothy 2:5, ESV

Jesus opened the door for you to have direct access to God through His sacrifice on the cross. If you have suffered under an abusive relationship I want to encourage you to forgive those who harmed you, and move on in your walk with God. Forgiveness is crucial to a healthy relationship with the Lord, and with other people.

I mentioned the Christian community that my family had been involved in, and the difficulties that arose because of immature leadership—and immature followership, too. A friend of ours from this community had suffered under this controlling leadership and was having a hard time letting go of his anger—particularly towards one specific leader. Not long after leaving this fellowship, he and his wife moved to another city to attend a Christian university. The Lord used this time in a different atmosphere to bring healing, but there was still one person he couldn't bring himself to forgive. He prayed for God to give him the grace to release his anger towards this person, but the feelings remained. After many months had passed he concluded that it would just take time for the wounds to heal, and he stopped worrying about it. But every once in a while the anger would rise up in his heart and he knew that he had not yet fully forgiven this leader.

After several months our friend went to a meeting to hear a Christian motivational speaker. The man spoke of friendship, fellowship, and forgiveness for your brother and sister in the Lord. Toward the end of his message, he told the audience it was important to be doers or the word, and not just hearers. "I want every other row to turn to the person behind them, take their hand and say, 'I love you, and I forgive you in Jesus' name.'" Our friend turned around and standing directly behind him was the very leader who he had such a hard time forgiving. Hesitantly he took her hand and could hardly get the words out of his mouth. After an awkward moment he finally said, "I love you, and I forgive you, in Jesus' name."

His feelings didn't immediately change, but at that moment God did a work in the spirit. Within a short time his emotions of anger began to dissipate and eventually they completely disappeared. This man graduated with honors from this Christian university and went on to serve the Lord in several ministries.

Godly counsel is an important part of how God leads us, but it is only one part. By filtering direction through all of the seven keys you can avoid some of the pitfalls that others have succumbed to. As you reject spiritually abusive relationships and walk in forgiveness you will find doors open for you that you might not expect. Remember, there is safety in the seven keys to God's guidance.

Questions for Meditation

1. List any persons to whom you are accountable. In what ways are you accountable? How does this accountability help you in living out the Christian life?

2. Read Exodus 18:13—27. What was the problem that Moses faced? What did his father-in-law tell him to do? What was the result?

> The next day, Moses took his seat to hear the people's disputes against each other. They waited before him from morning till evening. When Moses' father-in-law saw all that Moses was doing for the people, he asked, "What are you really accomplishing here? Why are you trying to do all this alone while everyone stands around you from morning till evening?"
>
> Moses replied, "Because the people come to me to get a ruling from God. When a dispute arises, they come to me, and I am the one who settles the case between the

quarreling parties. I inform the people of God's decrees and give them his instructions."

"This is not good!" Moses' father-in-law exclaimed. "You're going to wear yourself out—and the people, too. This job is too heavy a burden for you to handle all by yourself. Now listen to me, and let me give you a word of advice, and may God be with you. You should continue to be the people's representative before God, bringing their disputes to him. Teach them God's decrees, and give them his instructions. Show them how to conduct their lives. But select from all the people some capable, honest men who fear God and hate bribes. Appoint them as leaders over groups of one thousand, one hundred, fifty, and ten. They should always be available to solve the people's common disputes, but have them bring the major cases to you. Let the leaders decide the smaller matters themselves. They will help you carry the load, making the task easier for you. If you follow this advice, and if God commands you to do so, then you will be able to endure the pressures, and all these people will go home in peace."

Moses listened to his father-in-law's advice and followed his suggestions. He chose capable men from all over Israel and appointed them as leaders over the people. He put them in charge of groups of one thousand, one hundred, fifty, and ten. These men were always available to solve the people's common disputes. They brought the major cases to Moses, but they took care of the smaller matters themselves.

Soon after this, Moses said good-bye to his father-in-law, who returned to his own land.

—Exodus 18:13-27, NLT

3. Read Acts 16:1–5. What caused Paul to choose Timothy as a traveling companion?

> Paul went first to Derbe and then to Lystra, where there was a young disciple named Timothy. His mother was a Jewish believer, but his father was a Greek. Timothy was well thought of by the believers in Lystra and Iconium, so Paul wanted him to join them on their journey. In deference to the Jews of the area, he arranged for Timothy to be circumcised before they left, for everyone knew that his father was a Greek. Then they went from town to town, instructing the believers to follow the decisions made by the apostles and elders in Jerusalem. So the churches were strengthened in their faith and grew larger every day.
> —Acts 16:1-5, NLT

4. Write out Proverbs 20:18. What does this passage have to say about godly counsel?

> Plans succeed through good counsel; don't go to war without wise advice.
> —Proverbs 20:18, NLT

5. Read Matthew 23:4. What did Jesus have to say about the Pharisees? How can this passage help us to detect the presence of spiritual abuse?

> They crush people with unbearable religious demands and never lift a finger to ease the burden.
> —Matthew 23:4, NLT

6. What examples of spiritual abuse have you seen? It may have been in your church or another, by a pastor or a layperson.

7. Was your experience similar or dissimilar to the description of the Pharisees in the Bible?

Chapter Eight

Peace – Reaping the Fruit of Hearing God's Voice

> For the Kingdom of God is...living a life of goodness and peace and joy in the Holy Spirit.
> —Romans 14:17, NLT

eace and joy should be a natural part of your daily life as a Christian. But just like all the benefits of the kingdom of God, these attributes come at a price.

During the darkest days of the Revolutionary War, as George Washington tried to regroup during the winter of 1776, the great writer, Thomas Paine, wrote a stirring essay on a drumhead that encapsulated the monumental struggle of that conflict. It was called "The American Crisis," and it so moved George Washington that he ordered his officers to read it to every soldier in the Continental Army, hoping it would inspire them to not give up hope.

> These are the times that try men's souls. The summer soldier and the sunshine patriot will in this crisis shrink from the service of their country. But they that stand it now, deserve the love and thanks of men and women. Tyranny, like hell, is not easily conquered. But the harder the conflict, the more glorious the triumph. Heaven knows how to put a proper price on its goods. It would be strange indeed if so celestial an article as freedom should not be highly rated...[34]

It's the same with the other celestial articles, like peace, joy, and the other fruit and gifts of the Holy Spirit. Things of great value, both natural and spiritual, come at a great price.

Being a disciple of Jesus Christ is not easy. God's salvation may be free, but discipleship is costly. The gifts of the Spirit may also be freely given, but they are not cheap. Our preparation for God's eternal purpose is as rigorous, spiritually, as an Olympic athlete's training is naturally—even more so, because the outcome of our training has eternal ramifications. Learning to hear God's voice is a life-long process.

There's a scene in the movie *A League of Their Own* in which Gina Davis' character wants to quit the women's professional baseball team to be with her husband who has returned wounded from World War Two. Tom Hanks, who plays the manager of the team, tries to talk his star player into coming back for the remainder of the season. She begins

---

[34] Paine, Thomas. *The Crisis*. Good Reads
https://www.goodreads.com/quotes/175410-these-are-the-times-that-try-men-s-souls-the-summer

to cry at the thought of returning to the road with the baseball team and she protests that "...it's just so hard."

Tom Hanks character gets right in her face and spouts back at her, "Of course it's hard. It's the 'hard' that makes it great."

Our walk with the Lord is hard. There are some who find it so difficult that they want to give up and go back to the pleasures of the sinful life. But Jesus said,

> Anyone who puts a hand to the plow and then looks back is not fit for the Kingdom of God."
> —Luke 9:62, NLT

It's when we strive to hear His voice and obey His commands that we experience His joy and peace. And only then will we be the effective ministers He wants us to be—and that the world needs us to be.

Being Led Forth in Peace

Without great trials, we would have no great victories. The Lord reveals himself in the difficulties of life as our Deliverer and our Sufficiency. The psalmist tells us,

> Many are the afflictions of the righteous, but the Lord delivers him out of them all.
> —Psalm 34:19, NKJV

If you are serious about walking with God, He will teach you, and guide you, and comfort you, and yes, you will know His peace in your life. In fact, as you mature in your walk with the Lord, peace and joy will be multiplied to you. It's an interesting paradox that our Heavenly Father orchestrates in our lives. On the one hand our trials increase as we grow stronger in the Lord. On the other hand, the fruit of the

Spirit—including peace and joy—develop to the point that we are given grace to weather the trials, and the rest of our lives are filled with harmonious fellowship with God.

We should expect to experience God's peace in our lives. If you are not walking in peace it may be as a result of several different scenarios. It may be that you are in the midst of a particular test or trial sent from God. You may be under attack from the Devil. Or you may have an area of your life that you have not yet surrendered completely to God. The Lord intends for believers to live in peace—as much as is possible in this fallen world. So if you are not experiencing God's peace on an ongoing basis you may need to do some self-examination and reflection. Ask the Holy Spirit to show you:

- If you are experiencing a test that should be submittedto;

- If you are under an attack that you should resist; or

- If there is an area of continual sin, unforgiveness, anger, or some other hindrance that should be renounced and repented of.

When you are seeking God's will you can usually identify the leading of the Holy Spirit when you sense God's peace about a matter. The peace of God is one of the key indicators of God's guidance. Colossians 3:15 tells us to, "Let the peace of God rule in our hearts." Peace is the umpire of our heart, telling us if we are "safe" in God's will, or "out" of God's plan, following our own path or the deception of the Devil.

The prophet Isaiah wrote,

> For you will go out with joy and *be led forth with peace*...
> —Isaiah 55:12a, NASB, emphasis mine

God's best for our lives is that we will be "led forth in peace and joy." Have you ever heard someone say, "I'm not going to allow these circumstances to rob my joy?" In making this declaration they are being absolutely biblical—peace and joy are our possessions when we are born again. The only way that you will walk in unrest as a mature believer is if you allow circumstances or the Devil to rob you of your joy.

Larry Tomczak says, "You are the only being in the universe that can cause defeat in your life."[35]

You may say, "The Devil robbed my joy." But the truth of the statement is that the Devil attempted to rob you of your joy—he only succeeded if you allowed him to. The life of the Christian is one of peace and joy. The Bible declares:

> You will keep him in perfect peace, whose mind is stayed on You, because he trusts in You.
> —Isaiah 26:3, NKJV

You'll notice that the promise of peace carries with it a condition—to trust in God. Once again we come back to necessity of living a lifestyle of faith. Paul wrote to the Romans,

> For the mind set on the flesh is death, but the mind set on the Spirit is life and peace...
> —Romans 8:6, NASB

A carnally minded person is one who is self-interested, self-indulgent, and self-sufficient. There is no peace in the selfish life. The spiritually minded person puts God in the center of their life. It's from this attitude of surrender to the Lordship and headship of Jesus Christ that peace comes into our lives.

---

[35] Tomczak, Larry. Biblical Confessions to Increase Your Faith, audio cassette, 1998.

There are times when we are seeking the will of God, and we reach the point of decision where we experience supernatural peace. This is an important aspect of discerning between good and evil, and it comes by reason of use (Hebrews 5:14). The peace of God is like a gyroscope in our souls, leading us in the direction that the Holy Spirit intends for our lives.

At the same time, the mature Christian will recognize that there is another way that God uses the fruit of peace to direct our steps. As we surrender to the Lordship of Jesus Christ in our lives He brings us to a place where we experience His blessed peace on a regular basis. Instead of anxiety, anger, or depression, the peace of God becomes the normal state of mind for the Christian. I have a friend named Daryl, and when I meet him I usually ask how he's doing. In a declaration of our biblical position in Christ, he always quotes the famous hymn, "It is well with my soul."

If I am in Christ, it truly is well with my soul. I am at peace with God, and I should be walking in peace in this world. That's not to say that each one of us won't have our share of problems—and sometimes we will have even more difficulties because of the spiritual warfare that swirls about us. But because we are God's children, and His Spirit comforts us and guides us, we can be at peace in spite of the circumstances.

So as maturing believers, when we are seeking after God's plan for our life, we must also be sensitive to a lack of peace in a particular direction. This absence of God's peace in the form of anxiety, stress, anger, or confusion can also be a strong indicator, warning that we may be stepping out of the will of God. Just as the Lord will grant special peace to the believer when he or she discovers His plan, He will also remove His peace when a Christian strays away from His course for their lives.

A life of walking in the Spirit is a life of peace because Jesus Christ is the Prince of Peace. The natural man does not comprehend the things of God for they are spiritual in nature. The Greek word used for "natural man" is *psuechkes*, which means *soul*. The soul includes the mind, will, and emotions. Jesus said that those who worship God, or have a relationship with Him, must do so in spirit and truth (John 4:23). If we seek to know God first, then we will grow to know His will. We trust that our Father in Heaven is taking care of us, and this then brings great peace to our souls. We give our burdens to the Lord, and He gives us his peace. What a wonderful exchange.

Peace and the Seven Keys

The peace of God, in harmony with the other keys of God's guidance, is like today's digital receivers that lock onto a radio signal, insuring that you receive the message loud and clear.

- Through God's peace we can know if the Lord is using a particular Scripture to speak to us about guidance in our lives.

- the peace of God we can learn to differentiate between the voice of God, our own thoughts, the voice of the Devil, and the voice of the world.

- The Lord will give you peace when a prophet of God is speaking on His behalf, and He will withhold peace when a false prophet is speaking to you—or when a godly person is merely speaking from his or her own mind, and not from the Spirit of Christ.

- When seeking godly counsel, the Lord will provide peace when the advice being given is from Him, and He will often withhold His peace when that person is counseling outside of God's will. They may be giving you sound, and even biblical advice, but if it is not within God's will for you at that time in your life you will not sense the peace of God.

- The peace of God will often be the deciding confirmation, the inner witness of the Holy Spirit that cannot be ignored as you seek God's guidance. If you don't have the peace of God you may not be quite in the center of God's will, you may be ahead of God's timing, or you may be completely off track. Do not move forward in any perceived guidance until you have this defining confirmation of God's peace.

- The Holy Spirit will provide you with God's peace when a particular circumstance is an indicator of God's guidance. And He will remove His peace if a circumstance is not a part of the collection of indicators that God is using to move you toward His will for your life.

Of all the seven keys to hearing God's voice, peace and the Scriptures are the two keys that must be in evidence in every decision. The lack of God's peace is a clear indicator of a red or yellow light in your path. When you experience God's peace, after you have considered the other keys and you are confident of God's timing, you will then have a green light to proceed in God's plan for your life.

Peace and the Unfolding of God's Will

The will of God is not like a blueprint that you receive at some point in your life showing you exactly what God's plan will be for the remainder of your time on this planet. The will of God is revealed to us incrementally throughout our lives. Receiving direction from the Lord is in many ways dependent on your desire and tenacity in seeking it. Just as Jacob wrestled with God, unwilling to let Him go until he received a blessing, we must wrestle with God in a spiritual sense, not letting go until we receive His direction in our lives.

This divine struggle occurs repeatedly at key junctures in our walk with God.

God will not play religious games with you. His will for you won't make you miserable. He will use you in a way where you will excel because He designed you for that purpose. This will bring peace to you. When that peace lifts, you know that there is a shift in the will of God and you need to seek Him in prayer for the next stage in His plan.

The farther you get from God's best for you the louder those alarm bells will ring. Be careful that you stay alert to these warning signs. A person can ignore the prodding of the Holy Spirit to get you back on track with the Lord. If this continues—if someone dismisses the lack of peace in their lives as merely the anxiety of living—they can desensitize themselves to the moving of the Holy Spirit. Over time, this can cause a rift in your relationship with the Lord and it can lead to deception in your life.

Be careful to guard your walk with the Lord. If the peace of God is not dwelling on the inside of you—if you have allowed someone or something to rob you of your joy—find out why it's gone. If you need to repent of some sin, do so quickly. If you need to forgive someone who has wronged you, be quick about it. Then when you have done all that is in your power to walk in obedience to God's commands, ask the Lord to restore unto you the joy of your salvation (see Psalm 51:12).

Be Careful of False Peace

Everyone needs to be cautious of false peace that comes when a decision has finally been made. There is also a deceptive peace that is temporary and fleeting as we work through a decision. It may feel like permanent peace for a short while as you consider your choices, but soon that false peace will dissipate and you'll be left with an uneasiness until the right decision is made. The peace that comes from God will withstand the tests of time, changing circumstances, and even our own changing ideas.

Another form of false peace can come as a result of feeding our flesh. The word "happiness" is associated with the word "happening." People are *happy* because perceived good things are *happening* for them. One can be happy, yet not have true peace and joy. There are millions of happy people in the world who don't know Christ. They try to fill the void of their empty hearts with all manner of things, from false religion, to drugs, sex, relationships, and material possession. False peace is like a pain reliever that dulls our spiritual senses, even though the cause of the unrest has not been dealt with.

Many believers allow false peace to influence their walk with Christ. They have allowed their senses to be dulled through entertainment, drugs and alcohol, sex, money, parties, business pursuits, political power, relationships with friends—the list goes on and on. At one time they made a commitment to the Lord, but they have walked away and are no longer seeking Him. Some don't even want to hear His voice because they know that if they stopped to listen to the voice of God He would call them to repent.

This is dangerous ground. Be careful to keep short accounts with God. If you have sinned, repent quickly. Make things right with Him. If you have been wounded by someone forgive them quickly. Don't hold on to bitterness and unforgiveness. Left unattended, bitterness will consume you. It will destroy you physically, and it can even destroy your spiritual life.

Don't be hasty in making decisions. The peace of God will be there in a month or in a year if the direction you are following is truly from the Lord. If it's not, you may find yourself going back and forth between peace and unrest. If this is the case it's best to wait, if possible, until you have a sustained peace—especially in major decisions concerning things like your career, your marriage, your children, or a geographical move.

The peace that is from God is an everlasting peace.

We see an example of God using a lack of peace to lead the Apostle Paul in 2 Corinthians 2:12. The Lord had opened a door for ministry, but Paul had no peace because he couldn't find his ministry partner, Titus, who was supposed to meet him in Troas. We don't know why the Lord opened the door—perhaps it was to show Paul that this opportunity was there in Troas for a later time. Maybe Paul was going to send someone else to minister here. Perhaps the timing for ministry may not have been right. We see three of the seven keys at work here: the leading of the Spirit, circumstances, and a lack of peace. Paul did not have peace in his heart because he didn't know where Titus was. Without that peace, he did not go through an obviously open door of ministry.

Paul didn't take an open door in and of itself as guidance from the Lord, but merely as one factor among several to consider.

There are times when we won't have direction from God through all seven of the keys to hearing His voice. We may have two, three, or more, as was the case with Paul in Troas. But along with biblical confirmation, a key indicator is always the peace of God.

This portion of Scripture reveals a liberating concept of God's guidance. As the apostle Paul exemplified, we are not bound to walk through a perceived open door—even if it is of the Lord. That door may be open, but it may be open for someone other than you. Our responsibility is to weigh that open door against the other keys of God's guidance. This includes considering how this opportunity may jeopardize the other responsibilities God has already assigned to us— like looking after the Titus's in our life.

Something I have learned in more than thirty years of full-time ministry is that there are more open doors, more opportunities, and more people who need to hear the Word of God than I have energy or resources to fill on my own. We can't do it all ourselves. We have to concentrate on doing what God wants us to do, not what seems like a glaring need. When we stand before God, we will not be commended for our hard work. If Jesus says, "Well done, good and faithful servant," it will be because we truly were a servant—that is, we listened for the Master's voice and then *did what He told us to do*. Not every need constitutes a call. The peace of God can help us to differentiate between what is good, and what is best; between what is a need and what is truly the call of God for us.

Are You at Peace?

It may have been years since you have experienced true peace in your life. I encourage you to examine your life to determine if a change in career or circumstances is necessary. If you take a personality profile and find that your makeup does not match your career choice, you may want to investigate making a change. Don't do anything hastily, but seek the Lord for wisdom and then step out in faith as He directs your path.

You may have a lack of peace in your life for other reasons. In my years of ministry I have known many people who have been victims of physical, emotional, verbal, or sexual abuse. These are dear people who love God and truly want to hear His voice and follow His direction. But the pain from past hurts often clouds their ability to sense God's peace in their hearts, and makes it difficult to discern His leading in their lives.

If you are one of these hurting people, take heart. The Prince of Peace is able to heal your heart and bring His peace to your soul. It will take some effort on your part as the years of abuse may have left deep wounds. But wonderful ministries exist that work with victims of abuse. They can help you work through your pain and come to a place of forgiveness and peace in Christ. Talk to your pastor about a Christian counselor in your area, or look online for links to counseling ministries nationwide.

The bottom line is that God wants you to walk in peace—and He has given the fruit of peace to His children to act as a compass in our decision making. If you ask, the Holy Spirit will guide your steps, and will lead you out in His peace.

Questions for Meditation

1. How do you see the relationship between trust in God and peace in your life?

2. Have you ever had your peace upset by a proposition that was not from God? How did that feel? How did it affect your decision making process?

3. How has your relationship with God brought peace to your life?

4. How can the peace of God help to differentiate between the voice of God, our own thoughts, the voice of the Devil, and the voice of the world?

5. How can a lack of peace be a red or yellow light in your path?

6. In what ways do you need to begin practicing the presence of God in your daily life? How might that cause peace to multiply?

7. How can God's peace lead us in the timing of our decisions?

8. Why is an open door in itself not enough of a reason to make a decision?

CHAPTER NINE

PERSONAL PROPHECY - HEARING GOD'S SPECIFIC VOICE TO YOU

I was not having a good day.

I had made a request to have some video work done at the Christian television ministry where I worked. I needed it by 5 o'clock to meet a deadline. Somehow the order form was lost and the job wasn't done. The video wouldn't be ready until the next morning. So much for the deadline.

I was having difficulty maintaining my joy when suddenly one of my friends walked in the door and said with a smile, "Craig, here she is!" The "she" was one of the hosts of the national Christian talk show that this ministry produced. Earlier that day, my friend called and said she had a friend who was going through a difficult time. She asked if I would be willing to pray over her and see if the Lord had a prophetic word—but she didn't tell me who it was. I said, "Sure, I'd be happy to pray for her. Tell me where and when to meet you."

Several hours went by and I did not hear from her. And then my crisis emerged over the deadline and the needed video. Suddenly, in walks my friend with this nationally-known Christian celebrity. I was certainly not in the mood to pray over anyone at that moment, especially not someone of that stature. But I smiled and greeted them anyway.

"Do you have time right now to pray?"

"Sure," I responded, deciding to trust in God's promise that when we are weak, He is strong. "Just let me finish what I'm doing here and I'll be right with you." After I completed a new request form I rushed out to meet them. In my heart I quickly repented for my frustration and silently prayed what I always do before I minister:

> May the words of my mouth and the meditation of my heart be pleasing to you, O Lord, my rock and my redeemer.
> —Psalms 19:14, NLT

Another friend who has the gift of prophecy was in the hall and so I asked everyone if she could also join us, and they all agreed.

They led us into what is called the "green room," the place where guests sit and wait until they are led onto the set of the talk show. I shook my head at the thought of what was happening. Here I was in the green room of a national Christian talk show, getting ready to prophesy to this highly respected host. For a kid from Erie, Pennsylvania, it was spiritually heady stuff. "Lord, let what I say be from Your heart," I silently prayed.

As soon as we sat down I received a very detailed vision from the Lord. I saw this woman holding a baby in her arms, trying to protect it from a huge demon that was attacking them with a sword. The demon continually swung the sword at them, but an invisible force field was protecting them from the blows.

I had been trained in the prophetic ministry under Dr. Bill Hamon who cautioned to be careful about prophesying about major geographical moves, marriages, and babies. These are such highly-charged emotional issues that the minister needs to be careful not to put his own interpretation into what God may be saying.

Because the vision I had involved a baby, I decided to keep it to myself, concerned that it had just been my imagination. My friend prayed and prophesied over the young lady first, and then it was my turn.

There are different types of prophetic expressions that the Holy Spirit may give to a believer. Some people see scenarios unfolding in their mind. Others feel a physical sensation, especially when the Lord is giving them a word of knowledge about a healing. Some prophets receive a phrase and share just that, and then the Lord gives them another phrase, and so on. And then there are those who are called "Nabi" prophets, who just allow the words to flow from them in a stream of personal prophecy. I have more of a Nabi-like prophetic flow when I minister, although the Holy Spirit has given me all of these other types of revelations throughout the years as well.

I laid my hand on the young lady's forehead and immediately the vision once again flashed in front of my eyes, exactly as it had the first time—with the same details and intensity.

Having seen the vision a second time, I could not hold back from sharing it. "There are certain things that you need to be cautious of when you are ministering prophetically," I began tentatively. "I have been taught to be careful about giving prophecies concerning marriage, babies, and geographical moves. The Bible says to test all things and hold on to what is good. So I want to encourage you to carefully weigh what I am about to share with you." The young lady nodded her head soberly.

I paused and then began to describe the vision. "I saw you holding a baby in your arms..." I hadn't even finished the phrase when she burst into uncontrollable sobbing. I waited while her friend rubbed her shoulders, comforting the young woman.

After a few moments of crying she grew quiet again and I continued to describe what I saw. "You were holding a baby in her arms," I repeated, "trying to protect it from a huge demon that was attacking you both with a sword. The demon continually swung the sword at you, but an invisible force field was protecting you from the blows. The demon was enraged that he could not harm you or your child, and he kept hacking away to no avail. The whole time you were crying out, 'Why won't my husband come and defend us from this attack?' But your husband was nowhere to be found."

I told her that I sensed the Lord wanted to give them a child, but the enemy was attacking to try to thwart God's plan. I also sensed that the husband was not completely in agreement, and wasn't even walking in right relationship with the Lord. That was why he was not defending her against the demonic attack. I prayed for God's perfect will to be done in their lives and in this situation.

When I finished praying, the young lady wiped the tears from her eyes and told us that the prophetic words were accurate and timely. She had wanted to have a baby for some time, but her husband had been opposed to the idea. In the last year he had fallen away from the Lord and was seeking worldly pursuits.

But in the past few weeks he had come around and was now open to the idea of having children. In fact, she thought she might have been pregnant, but she had just started her period and was concerned that she may have lost the baby.

We prayed for her marriage, for her husband, and that the Lord would knit the two of them together in love for each other and for God. Then we prayed that they would be blessed with a child at the right time.

A couple weeks later I saw the host after chapel and she gave me a giant hug. "I just found out that I'm pregnant!" she exclaimed.

"Praise the Lord!" I responded

"And not only that," she added with a big smile. "The doctor said I have been pregnant for more than three months. That means that I was pregnant when you prophesied over me. Maybe the fact that I thought I was having my period was a sign of the attack that Satan was waging against the baby and me?"

"God is the bomb!" she declared.

I couldn't agree with her more.

Prophecy and The 7 Keys

Every day we are faced with difficult decisions. Those who have asked Jesus to be Lord over their lives desire to know they are walking in the will of God at they make these decisions. The Bible gives us principles and general instructions for how to live our lives. But when it comes to making specific decisions about critical areas of our lives, Scripture is not always able to speak precisely to our situation.

As we have explained, God can communicate with us through the Bible, and also directly to our heart through the Holy Spirit. As he did with Adam and Eve in the cool of the day, God desires to have a daily, personal relationship with each of His children. But sadly, not all Christians understand how to recognize the voice of the Lord. Or they may be seeking to hear God's voice, but they are under pressure in making their decision.

Even Christians who know how to hear God's voice at times may not respond to the Lord in a biblical manner. Sometimes the circumstances of life can be so stressful and confusing that a believer needs outside confirmation to know for certain what God is saying to them. Personal prophecy is one of the keys of God's guidance that can bring that confirmation.

Personal prophecy, tested along with the other keys, can help believers make important decisions in life. No Christian is self-sufficient—we are all a part of the Body of Christ. The only way we can live a fruitful and productive Christian life is to be an active member of a thriving community of believers in a local church. I have seen in my own life that sometimes the Lord will purposely withhold information to force me to seek godly counsel and confirmation of His leading through others. This keeps me interconnected and accountable. Through prophets and other Christians in the local church who flow in the gift of prophecy the Lord can speak to us and direct our steps.

Some may ask, "Is it scriptural to seek God's guidance through personal prophecy? Is it proper for a Christian to go to a prophet and expect to receive a specific prophetic word of direction, instruction, or confirmation?" The answer is yes—but like all the keys of God's guidance, that word must be judged against the Scripture and confirmed through peace, and in the mouth of two or three witnesses before it is acted upon.

Throughout the Bible we see God speaking to His saints through the prophets. In fact, through the prophet Amos the Lord declares:

> Surely the Lord God does nothing unless He reveals His secret to His servants the prophets. A lion has roared! Who will not fear? The Lord God has spoken! Who can but prophesy?"
> —Amos 3:7-8, NKJV

We see dozens of prophets operating under the leading of the Holy Spirit in both the Old and New Testaments. Beyond these, the Bible shows that other believers moved in the gifts of prophecy, word of knowledge, word of wisdom, discerning of spirits, and the prophetic song of the Lord through the power of the Holy Spirit.

Prophets are even in action in the biblical Last Days. The apostle John writes in the book of Revelation that in the last days God will raise up two mighty prophets who will do signs and wonders in the name of the Lord (Rev. 11:3 and 6).

If the ministry of the prophet is no longer needed by the church because the Bible has replaced them (as some would teach, quoting 1 Corinthians 13:10) then why do we find them functioning in the end times, long after the canon was completed? Why is there a record of prophecy from the time of the church fathers, through the dark ages, the Reformation, the Pentecostal movement, and even today? In fact, there seems to be an acceleration of prophetic activity in the Church today as we draw nearer to the time of Jesus' return.

The Apostle Paul wrote of Jesus:

> ...He Himself gave some to be apostles, some prophets, some evangelists, and some pastors and teachers, for the equipping of the saints for the work of ministry... 'till we all come to the unity of the faith and of the knowledge of the Son of God, to a perfect man, to the measure of the stature of the fullness of Christ...
>
> —Ephesians 4:11-13, NKJV

We observe in this passage that these gifts—including the gift of the prophet—are given *until* "we all come to the unity of the faith ... to the measure of the stature of the fullness of Christ." My question to those who say the gift of prophecy and the office of the prophet did not continue past the First Century is, "have contemporary Christians come into the unity of the faith and to the measure of the stature of the fullness of Christ?" The obvious answer is no. So when do you think we will attain this unity and fullness of stature? Again, most people would answer, "When Jesus returns." So then it follows that the gift of prophecy and the office of the prophet—along with the other gifts and offices—remain in full effect until Jesus returns.

The canonization of the Scriptures into the 66 books of the Bible did not eliminate the need for prophets in the church. And unlike Old Testament times where one prophet walked in God's anointing, today millions of people across the globe have the Holy Spirit residing on the inside and can prophecy at His leading. God can speak to and through any believer who is willing to be used as His vessel.

This is God's promise spoken by Peter on the Day of Pentecost regarding His people in the last days—which most theologians and Christian leaders agree refers to the days leading up to the return of Jesus:

> And it shall come to pass in the last days, says God, that *I will pour out My Spirit on all flesh*; your sons and your daughters *shall prophesy*, your young men *shall see visions*, your old men *shall dream dreams*. And on My menservants and on My maidservants I will pour out My Spirit in those days; and *they shall prophesy*.
> —Acts 2:17-18, NKJV, emphasis mine

The promise of the Holy Spirit dwelling within and moving in power through men and women is open to anyone who has faith to receive it! That is why the Apostle Paul declared these things to the church in Corinth:

> ...whenever you come together, each of you has a psalm, has a teaching, has a tongue, has a revelation, has an interpretation. Let all things be done for edification.
>
> —1 Corinthians 14:26, NKJV

> ...you can all prophesy one by one, that all may learn and all may be encouraged.
>
> —1 Corinthians 14:31, NKJV

> ...the manifestation of the Spirit is given to each one for the profit of all.
>
> —1 Corinthians 12:7, NKJV

The manifestation of the Spirit that Paul speaks of here is the same promise that Peter spoke of in Acts 2 and Joel 2—the Holy Spirit being poured out upon all flesh. The only thing we need to do to in response is to believe that God wants to use us to demonstrate His love and power to lost people in the world—and then to act upon that belief!

One of the ways God helps believers grow into a place of maturity is through the ministry of the *New Testament Office of the Prophet*. Through the manifestation of the Holy Spirit, He has also established the *gift of prophecy* to communicate in the local church. And as He inhabits the praises and prayer times of His people, He releases *the spirit of prophecy* to any disciple of Jesus Christ to give testimony to His Lordship in the earth today! Through all of these channels, God communicates His message of love to the world.

Dr. Bill Hamon defines prophecy as:

> ...simply God communicating His thoughts and intents to mankind. When a true prophecy is given, the Holy Spirit inspires someone to communicate God's pure and exact words to the individual or group for whom they are

intended. It is delivered without any additions or subtractions by the one prophesying, including any applications or interpretations suggested by the one speaking. To be most effective, it must also be delivered in God's timing and with the proper spirit or attitude.[36]

The Bible makes it clear that prophecy is a most powerful gift, and it is encouraged throughout the Scriptures. In 1 Corinthians 14:1 the Apostle Paul writes:

> Pursue love, yet desire earnestly spiritual gifts, but especially that you may prophesy.
> —1 Corinthians 14:1, NASB

Then later in verse 39, he declares:

> Therefore, brethren, desire earnestly to prophesy...
> —1 Corinthians 14:39, NASB

The phrase "desire earnestly" comes from the Greek word *zeloo*, which means to have great desire, to be jealous over, and to be zealously affected. It implies fervency of mind, and even an emotional jealousy as a husband would have towards his wife—an intense hunger to hear from God. Paul is encouraging Christians to have this kind of desire to give and receive personal prophecy and to see the gifts of the Spirit manifested in the church.

Prophecy is not only for a corporate gathering of believers, but the Lord uses this precious gift to speak directly to individuals as He wills. The Bible is clear that believers are to desire earnestly—some translations say *covet*—the

---

[36] Hamon, Bill. *Prophets and Personal Prophecy*, Shippensburg, PA: Destiny Image Publishers, page 29.

prophetic ministry. In fact, it is the only ministry the Bible tells us we *are* to covet.

Edification, Exhortation, and Comfort

Prophecy in the New Testament is used by God to speak edification, exhortation, and comfort to individual believers, and also to small groups, local churches, the church in a particular geographical area, and sometimes, to the entire Body of Christ (see 1 Cor. 14:3). Another word for edification is "up-building," which is the Greek word *oikodome*, meaning "to build a house." Prophecy is to be used to build up the household of believers by communicating the heart and thoughts of God.

Jesus uses the term *Paraclete* in the Gospel of John to refer to the Holy Spirit. The apostle Paul uses the same root word for "encouragement" in 1 Corinthians 14:3; *paraclesis*. Through prophecy, the Holy Spirit encourages us in our Christian walk. He also exhorts us to fulfill all of God's will for our lives by His power and grace.

"To encourage" is to speak words that drive away fear, and build faith or "courage" in our hearts. That is what the Holy Spirit often does through personal prophecy.

Paul uses the Greek word *paramuthia* for "comfort" in this passage, which means to exercise a gentle influence of consolation. The Holy Spirit will calm our fears and bring peace to our hearts through a prophetic word spoken in a gracious manner.

But be careful to guard yourself against a prophetic word given in a harsh, judgmental, condescending, or critical manner. The New Covenant prophet gives words under the grace of Jesus Christ, through edification, exhortation, and comfort—not criticism or judgment.

Prophets are used to vocalize the revelation of God as well as provide specific instruction for individual lives. New Testament prophecy is only one of the seven keys of God's guidance—but it is an important key that should not be overlooked. In his important book, *Prophets and Personal Prophecy*, Dr. Bill Hamon writes:

> God still wants the revelation of His will to be vocalized. So He has established the prophetic ministry as a voice of revelation and illumination which will reveal the mind of Christ to the human race. He also uses this ministry to give specific instructions to individuals concerning His personal will for their lives.
>
> The ministry of the prophet is not, of course, to bring about additions or subtractions to the Bible. Any new additions accepted as infallibly inspired would be counterfeits, false documents which would contain delusions that lead to damnation. Instead, the prophet brings illumination and further specifics about that which has already been written. And the Holy Spirit's gift of prophecy through the saints is to bring edification, exhortation, and comfort to the Church (1 Corinthians. 14:3).[37]

The Lord's desire is to communicate directly to the heart of the individual believer. But the messages a person believes is from God must be confirmed in the mouth of two or three witnesses (see Deut. 19:15; 1 Cor. 13:1). One of the ways the

---

[37] Ibid, p. 13.

vital function of confirmation can be fulfilled is through personal prophecy.

The prophet, along with personal prophecy, should never to take the place of the voice of the Holy Spirit within the heart of a believer. Prophets are an extension of the ministry of the Holy Spirit in communicating the mind of Christ to the Church. As such, it is just as scriptural for Christians to seek guidance, confirmation, and insights into God's will through a prophet or prophetic presbytery as it is to seek directive counseling from a pastor. God approves of this practice as long as we don't allow personal prophecy to become a substitute for hearing the voice of God in our own times of prayer, searching the Scriptures, fasting, and seeking His face.

We must seek the Lord through all the keys to God's guidance. But from time to time when we need the Lord to speak to a specific area of our lives, and we have been diligent in seeking His will in our personal times of prayer, we can seek personal prophecy as another means of discovering His plan for our lives.

Speaking of the gift of prophecy and the manifestation of the Holy Spirit in the Church, the apostle Paul wrote,

> But be sure that everything is done properly and in order.
>
> —1 Corinthians 14:40, NLT

Some Charismatic or Pentecostal Christians may cry out, "Let all things be done!" While other Evangelical or Mainline Christians may declare, "Decently and in order!" But the Lord wants to bring the Church into balance regarding the gifts of the Spirit to "let all things be done—decently and in order."

It's true there have been abuses of personal prophecy. There are false prophets and false prophecies in the world today—just as God warned there would be wolves in sheep's clothing (Matt. 7:15). But that is not a reason to stand in the way of what God wants to do in and through His people in prophetic communication. When natural fire spreads outside of its proper boundaries it can cause death and destruction—but that doesn't hinder us from using fire as the blessing that God intended it to be to heat our homes and cook our food. Personal prophecy has sometimes been improperly used in ways that hurt people, but that should not hinder the Church from allowing it to be expressed within its proper biblical boundaries to bring life, joy, and freedom.

God is a Creator. Satan is an imitator. For every true, genuine gift of God there will be a counterfeit. In a way, knowing there is a demonic forgery of the gift of prophecy should encourage our faith to believe God for the real. If the Devil can promote psychics, witches, astrologers, and the like, then we know that God has prophets speaking on His behalf in the world today!

As we have shown, Paul's test of prophecy given to the Thessalonian Church is vital guide for judging personal prophecy:

> Do not *quench the Spirit*; do not *despise prophetic utterances*. But examine everything carefully; hold fast to that which is good.
> —1 Thessalonians 5:19-21, NASB, emphasis mine

There is a dual implication in verse 21. First of all, if we can hold fast to what is good, then Paul is telling us that personal prophecy is a good thing. The second implication is that if we are to test all things and hold fast to what is good, then not everything that you will hear in a personal prophecy is good. In these cases we should weigh the prophetic word against the other keys, then as they say, "eat the meat and spit out the bones."

The word "despise" in this passage is from the Greek word *exoudenoo*, which means "to make utterly nothing of." The apostle Paul is exhorting believers that they should not "make utterly nothing of" the gift of prophecy in their lives. The Lord intends for believers to receive personal prophecy in their life in faith, but to do so in a biblically balanced manner, with proper spiritual oversight. When we do this, we unlock the door to tremendous blessing both for us, our families, our churches—and through us, the world.

Personal Prophecy is Partial and Progressive

In order to properly incorporate personal prophecy into our lives we must understand that it will always be partial, progressive, and conditional. Paul declared that

> ...we know in part and we prophesy in part.
> —1 Corinthians 13:9, NASB

Personal prophecy is partial in that God only reveals what we need to know in order to do His will in a particular area of our lives. Personal prophecy is only a small insight into God's overall will for our lives. A prophecy may only speak to a certain "chapter" of our life story. Knowing that prophecy is partial helps us to understand that just because the Lord doesn't speak about a certain area of our lives, that doesn't mean that He doesn't want us to move forward in that thing if we have been led through the other keys of God's guidance.

Often the Lord only gives us a small glimpse into His plan for us because He doesn't want to overwhelm us with what the future may hold. He also desires that we continue to come to Him seeking our daily bread. He seems to give that bread one or two slices at a time for our protection and peace of mind.

In my own experience the Lord never spoke a single thing through prophecy concerning my writing ministry until I already had a contract for my first book. For years I pursued higher education, writing jobs, and book ideas based only on a burning desire in my heart to write, and an assurance that such a pursuit was biblical. I believed the Lord had sanctioned my writing by speaking to my heart that He wanted me to be a journalist. But it wasn't until just a few weeks before my first book was to be published that I received my first prophetic word that God wanted to use my writing to be a blessing to the Body of Christ.

Because I knew that personal prophecy was only one of the seven keys, I didn't allow the fact that God had not confirmed a writing ministry through the prophetic to hinder me from developing this part of the call on my life. The desire in my heart was actually the motivating factor, leading me forward in my writing career. Needless to say, it was reassuring and exciting when God confirmed this calling through a personal prophecy. But by that time I had already earned an MA in journalism and had worked as a writer and Internet producer for many years.

Now the Lord had spoken quite a bit about other areas of my life through personal prophecy, especially regarding my call to full time ministry. These words have been confirming, and even directional at times, but they have always been encouraging and comforting, and they have exhorted me to press on in my relationship with the Lord.

Besides being partial, personal prophecy is also progressive. The Lord will unfold and reveal His will through prophecy gradually over a lifetime, with each prophetic word adding new information and revelation. For this reason, time is often the greatest trial of faith for believing the promises of the Lord given to us through personal prophecy.

Abraham and Sarah had to wait twenty-five years for the fulfillment of God's prophecy about Isaac—and they were already elderly when the promise first came to them. The apostle Paul had to wait years before the prophecy of his ministry to the gentiles would be fulfilled. King David waited for nearly twenty years between the time he was anointed as king by Samuel and the time he actually ascended to the throne. Joseph received his prophetic dream when he was a teenager, but more than twenty years had passed before he saw a fulfillment of God's revelation in his life.

Only For Confirmation?

There are some who teach that personal prophecy is only for confirmation and can never be directional. There is no verse in the Bible that says this. In fact, Scripture shows numerous examples of directive personal prophecy as we have already pointed out. Of course, all directional prophetic words must line up with Scripture and be confirmed through the other keys.

The late Demos Shakarian, founder of *The Full Gospel Business Men's Fellowship*, shared an amazing example of a directional prophecy that changed the course of his life.

The Shakarian family lived in the village of Kara Kala in Armenia, at the foot of Mount Ararat. All of them were Christians, having received the Gospel through the witness of Russian Orthodox believers at the end of the nineteenth century. In his village there lived an 11-year-old illiterate boy whose name was Efim. One day this lad heard the Lord calling him to a time of prayer and fasting. After seven days and nights, the Lord gave him a vision:

> Efim could neither read nor write. Yet, as he sat in the little stone cottage in Kara Kala, he saw before him a vision of charts and a message in a beautiful handwriting. Efim asked for pen and paper. And for seven days, sitting at the rough plank table where the family ate, he laboriously copied down the form and shape of letters and diagrams that passed before his eyes.
>
> When he had finished, the manuscript was taken to people in the village who could read. It turned out that this illiterate child had written out in Russian characters a series of instructions and warnings. At some unspecified time in the future, the boy wrote, every Christian in Kara Kala would be in terrible danger.
>
> He foretold a time of unspeakable tragedy for the entire area, when hundreds of thousands of men, women, and children would be brutally murdered. The time would come,

he warned, when everyone in the region must flee. They must go to a land across the sea. Although he had never seen a geography book, the boy prophet drew a map showing exactly where the fleeing Christians were to go. To the amazement of the adults, the body of water depicted so accurately in the drawing was not the nearby Black Sea, or the Caspian Sea, or even the farther off Mediterranean Sea, but the distant and unimaginable Atlantic Ocean! There was no doubt about it, nor about the identity of the land on the other side; the map plainly indicated the east coast of the United States of America.

But the refugees were not to settle down there, the prophecy continued. They were to continue traveling until they reached the west coast of the new land. There, the boy wrote, God would bless them and prosper them, and cause their seed to be a blessing to the nations.

More than 50 years passed and Efim, then an aging man, announced to the village the time had come to obey the prophecy. In response, the Shakarians, along with several other families, sold their goods and moved to America. Many of the other villagers did not heed the prophecy. Not long after this, in 1914, the Turks began a genocide that killed more than one million Armenians, including every single person in the village of Kara Kala.

The Shakarian family obeyed the word of the Lord and settled in California, where they started what would become a hugely successful dairy farm. As the prophecy foretold, the family prospered in this new land. Later, at the leading of the Holy Spirit, Demos Shakarian founded *The Full Gospel Business Men's Fellowship*, a ministry that eventually touched the lives of millions of people in America and around the world—fulfilling the prophecy that their seed would be a blessing to the nations.[38]

The Bible tells us:

> Believe in the Lord your God, and you will be established; believe His prophets, and you will succeed.
> —2 Chronicle. 20:20, ESV

I have received prophecies at times that were not only directional, but they were extremely challenging. They made me wonder how the Lord would ever do the things promised within it for me. The amazing thing is that many of those words that I thought were so huge have already come to pass in my life. God is well able to fulfill the word He speaks to us, but we are required to believe and act on these promises in faith.

The bottom line is that personal prophecy is a gift that Christ has given to the Church, but it should never replace our need to have an ongoing, personal relationship with God in which we hear His voice for ourselves.

Questions For Meditation

1. How can personal prophecy, along with the other keys to God's guidance, help a person to make decisions about God's will in their life?

2. Read 1 Corinthians 14:1, 39. What are we to desire earnestly"?

---

[38] Sherrill, John and Elizabeth, *The Happiest People on Earth*, Grand Rapids, MI, Chosen Books, 1975, pp. 19-20.

> Let love be your highest goal! But you should also desire the special abilities the Spirit gives—especially the ability to prophesy... So, my dear brothers and sisters, be eager to prophesy, and don't forbid speaking in tongues.
>
> —1 Corinthians 14:1, 39, NLT

3. Read 1 Corinthians 12:7–11. Why do you think God wants us to covet to prophesy?

   > A spiritual gift is given to each of us so we can help each other. To one person the Spirit gives the ability to give wise advice; to another the same Spirit gives a message of special knowledge. The same Spirit gives great faith to another, and to someone else the one Spirit gives the gift of healing. He gives one person the power to perform miracles, and another the ability to prophesy. He gives someone else the ability to discern whether a message is from the Spirit of God or from another spirit. Still another person is given the ability to speak in unknown languages, while another is given the ability to interpret what is being said. It is the one and only Spirit who distributes all these gifts. He alone decides which gift each person should have.
   >
   > —1 Corinthians 12:7-11, NLT

4. Write out 1 Thessalonians 5:19-21. What can we learn about how to respond to personal prophecy in this passage?

   > Do not stifle the Holy Spirit. Do not scoff at prophecies, ut test everything that is said. Hold on to what is good.
   >
   > —1 Thessalonians 5:19-21, NLT

5. How can a person quench the Spirit or despise prophecies?

6. How can you avoid quenching the Spirit or despising prophecies?

7. Write out 1 Corinthians 14:39-40. What does this passage show us about responding to personal prophecy?

> So, my dear brothers and sisters, be eager to prophesy, and don't forbid speaking in tongues. But be sure that everything is done properly and in order.
> —1 Corinthians 14:39-40, NLT

8. Read Deuteronomy 18:9-14 and Leviticus 19:31. Why do you think God's judgment of psychic practices is so severe?

> When you enter the land the Lord your God is giving you, be very careful not to imitate the detestable customs of the nations living there. For example, never sacrifice your son or daughter as a burnt offering. And do not let your people practice fortune-telling, or use sorcery, or interpret omens, or engage in witchcraft, or cast spells, or function as mediums or psychics, or call forth the spirits of the dead. Anyone who does these things is detestable to the Lord. It is because the other nations have done these detestable things that the Lord your God will drive them out ahead of you. But you must be blameless before the Lord your God. The nations you are about to displace consult sorcerers and fortune-tellers, but the Lord your God forbids you to do such things.
> —Deuteronomy 18:9-14, NLT

> Do not defile yourselves by turning to mediums or to those who consult the spirits of the dead. I am the Lord your God.
> —Leviticus 19:31, NLT

9. How does knowing that psychics pull from the *psuche* affect your view of their powers?

10. How can transcribing and meditating on a personal prophecy help you to better understand what God may be speaking to you?

11. Why is it important to weigh a personal prophecy against the other keys to hearing God's voice?

CHAPTER TEN

CONFIRMATION - HEARING GOD AGAIN AND AGAIN

ord, please confirm somehow what I am sensing you are saying to me..." This is one of my most repeated prayers.

The Apostle Paul declared:

...by the mouth of two or three witnesses every word shall be established.

—2 Corinthians 13:1, NKJV

This principle originated in the Old Testament, was confirmed by Christ, and then was repeated in several places in the New Testament.

Moses established the principle in the book of Deuteronomy:

> A single witness shall not rise up against a man on account of any iniquity or any sin which he has committed; on the evidence of two or three witnesses a matter shall be confirmed.
>
> —Deuteronomy 19:15, NASB

Jesus spoke of it in the Gospels:

> Even in your law it has been written that the testimony of two men is true.
>
> —John 8:17, NASB

> But if he does not listen to you, take one or two more with you, so that by the mouth of two or three witnesses every fact may be confirmed.
>
> —Matthew 18:16, NASB

Paul also referred to the practice:

> Do not receive an accusation against an elder except on the evidence of two or three witnesses.
>
> —1 Timothy 5:19, NASB

As I have said, our Father in heaven is willing and able to confirm His direction in our life. Not only that, but I believe He desires to confirm it for His glory, and so that you will know for a certainty that you are hearing His voice.

How Does God Confirm His Guidance?

I have found this old saying to be true about God's direction: "If God appoints, He anoints. If He calls, He equips. And what God orders, He pays for."

We can trust that if God calls us to do something difficult on behalf of His kingdom, He will supply us with all we need to accomplish His will in our lives—if we are humbly following Him.

There is a cacophony of voices in this world vying for our ear. Many people claim to speak on behalf of God. How can we know which voice is truly the Good Shepherd, and which is not?

God spoke to His people in Bible times, and there is no indication in Scripture that He has stopped speaking to His people today. On the day of Pentecost the Holy Spirit was poured out on the disciples, and the promise of Joel chapter two was fulfilled (Acts 2:17-18). There is nowhere in Scripture or in the history of the Church to indicate that the Lord has rescinded the gifts of the Holy Spirit—they are available to the believer today just as they were in the first century.

The God of the Bible is a God of order, and He will reveal the truths from His Word to help us to grow in Christ. Having said that, however, it's important to understand that God is God, and He can reveal His will to us in any way that He chooses to do so. Because He loves us, and because He does things in an orderly fashion, God will most often confine Himself to the ways that He has dealt with mankind throughout the ages as revealed in the Bible. We must be careful, however, to not put God into a box. He alone is God, and all that we know of Him is what He has chosen to reveal through His Word. I can tell you about the hundred and one ways that God has led His people in the Scriptures, and He can come up with a thousand and one different ways that He will lead you into His will for your life. Being God, He has that right.

If God in His sovereign will decides to do something differently, He's not limited by the principles in this book. But rest assured, typically He leads us through the seven keys. This is established in Scripture, and I've found it to be true in life.

I should also add that God will move supernaturally in the life of the Spirit filled believer, especially if you are crying out to Him for direction, and extending your faith to believe that He will reveal Himself. If you ask for Jesus to lead you, He will lead you.

When you ask for the Holy Spirit, you're going to get the Holy Spirit. Jesus said it this way:

> You fathers—if your children ask for a fish, do you give them a snake instead? ... Of course not! So if you sinful people know how to give good gifts to your children, how much more will your heavenly Father give the Holy Spirit to those who ask him.
>
> —Luke 11:11-12a, 13, NLT

Our Heavenly Father is not going to allow the Devil to play some kind of trick on you. When you sincerely ask God to direct your path, and you are doing all you can to walk in obedience to Him, He will be faithful to answer your prayer. You can take that to the bank!

Guided by the Desires of Our Hearts

The psalmist wrote,

> May He grant you according to your heart's desire, and fulfill all your purpose.
>
> —Psalm 20:4, NKJV

The Lord gives us wonderful promises like this one throughout His Word concerning the desire of our hearts. Just like an earthly father who delights in providing his children with the things they write on their Christmas list, our Heavenly Father delights in giving us the things we desire—but not all of them.

There are times when we desire something that seems good to us, but from God's point of view it may not be ultimately good for us. Or it may be good, but not His best.

Our Father in heaven truly knows what is best for our lives. There are times when we want certain things that He knows would be a hindrance to us and so He will withhold them from us.

There is such a thing as a divine rejection. There are times when we cry out to God, "Lord, this is the desire of my heart! Please give it to me." But the Father knows that the thing is actually bait on a sharp hook. If we were to swallow that bait it would entrap us and take us to places we do not want to go. In His love, God may withhold certain things to protect us.

In other cases there are things we desire that may not be at all harmful, but the Lord will keep them from us because He has something in store for us that is even better than we could imagine.

How many of us have prayed to be in a certain job, or marry a certain person, or receive a certain material blessing only to realize later that the job, person, or thing was not all that we thought it was. Many times when the Lord has withheld something from me, I have later come to realize that it was for my protection and my long-term good. It is always best to pray for God's will to be done, rather than just eagerly pursuing our own agenda.

It's also important to realize that sometimes the Lord will plant His desires in our heart and then cause those desires to grow so we will seek Him. At some point in the process He may require that we surrender those dreams back to Him. This is called "dying to the vision," and it's a test that the Lord will often guide His children through to determine their love for Him.

God may promise something to us and place a desire for it in our heart, and then He will require the very thing that He promised from us. We all remember the test that Abraham faced when God promised him an heir in his old age. The birth of this baby brought so much joy to Abraham and Sarah that they named him Isaac, which means laughter. When Isaac was a teenager the Lord tested Abraham's faith by asking him to offer his son as a sacrifice. In obedience, Abraham built an altar, placed the wood in order, bound the hands of his son and laid him on it. Just as he raised the knife to slay his son the angel of the Lord stopped him. God provided a ram caught in the thicket for Abraham and Isaac to sacrifice to the Lord (see Gen. 22).

If we are willing die to the vision that is in our heart and allow the Lord to have everything in our lives, He will not only give us the thing that He promised in the end, but it will be better than what we could have ever imagined in our own minds.

Corrie Ten Boom often spoke these words of wisdom:

Hold loosely to the things of this life, so that if God requires them of you it will be easy to let them go.[39]

God will give us the desires of our heart, but our first desire should be serving Christ Himself. When we have Jesus as our chief desire, we will submit all of the other desires of our heart to His Lordship, and then we can pray, "Not my will, but thine be done." When this happens, God will give us our hearts' desire, which will also be His desire for us!

When things don't seem to be working out, or you're having a difficult time, it's not always because you're out of the will of God. It may be that you are directly in His will and He is controlling the circumstances to bring about His purpose for you. In these times you must remain prayerful and consider the combination of ways He is guiding you. There are multiple Christians around the world who are wasting their lives doing nothing of significance as they wait for God to clearly reveal their calling to them. God has given them the Scripture, which reveals God's general will for all believers. In that alone they can see that the Lord does not want them to bury their talents, but instead use them to His glory (Matthew 25:14-30).

When Moses questioned God in front of the burning bush he said,

> ...What if they won't believe me or listen to me? What if they say, 'The Lord never appeared to you'?"
>
> —Exodus 4:1, NLT

---

[39] Ten Boom, Corrie, "A Faith Not Hidden," interview with Pat Robertson, The 700 Club, Christian Broadcasting Network, 1974.

The Lord replied to him,

> What is that in your hand?
>
> —Exodus 4:2, NLT

Of course we know it was the rod that the Lord used as an instrument to demonstrate His power.

The Lord is asking you today, "What is in your hand?" You may have read in the Bible that the Lord has a unique calling for your life. You may have heard some specific direction from the Lord concerning that calling. But are you still waiting for God to make it happen? It may be that God is waiting for you to step out in faith and act on what He has revealed to you.

I ask you today, "What is in your hand?" Do that which is at hand to do. Move forward in faith in the things you have heard from the Lord and God will meet you where you are. Like Peter in the boat on that stormy night you may have heard the voice of the Lord saying, "Come out on the water." You have to make a decision to lift your foot over the edge of that boat and step out, trusting that you have heard His voice, and keeping your eyes on Him in the midst of the storm. God will provide you with the grace and strength that you need to get it done, but you must take that first step in obeying His will for your life.

Hindrances to Confirmation

I once read a book by a major Christian leader who had fallen into moral failure and lost his ministry and his family as a result. As he sat in prison, paying for his mistakes, he decided to take some correspondence Bible college courses. After several months of study he came to the conclusion that one of the leading reasons for his downfall was that he had followed after popular teaching without properly searching the Scripture to see if it was actually God's truth. By floating along on the "winds of doctrine" he floated right into a series of ungodly relationships, which led to ungodly decisions, which in turn led to ungodly behavior. All of this led to the ultimate collapse of this man's life and ministry.

This dangerous practice is called proof-texting, which is the practice of looking for a particular phrase or passage of Scripture that seems to line up with our own previously-held belief, and then to pull it out of context and use it to justify that idea. This is an unhealthy approach to biblical interpretation and it can get us into trouble. In the case of this man, it led him into a series of disastrous circumstances.

Thankfully this minister learned from his mistakes and is now out of prison, remarried, and serving the Lord once again. Thank God for His faithfulness—

> Though they stumble, they will never fall, for the Lord holds them by the hand.
> —Psalms 37:24, NLT

Another major hindrance to properly confirming the direction of the Lord is trying to hear what we want to hear, rather than truly being open to the Lordship of Jesus Christ in our decisions. George Muller was the leader of a large orphanage in England. He was a mighty spiritual intercessor and during his prayer times he received specific guidance from the Lord. Someone once asked him the secret of receiving such clear direction from heaven. He replied, "Have no mind of your own in the matter."

When you want to know the will of God for your life it's best to come to the Lord with no agenda of your own. You should have no preconceived notions and no position to advocate before God. If you want to truly be led by the Lord you shouldn't come into your time of prayer with a to-do list for which you want God's help. Instead, you should ask the Lord what He wants you to do, listen for His voice, and obey His leading.

In other words, instead of always asking for God's blessing on what we are doing, we should get in the habit of praying that we would be doing what God is blessing.

Known by the Friends You Keep

As Paul declared:

> Bad company corrupts good character.
> —1 Corinthians 15:33, NIV

It's important that we surround ourselves with people of godly character. We can be just as unequally yoked in our friendships as we can be in our marriage. We can be hindered in seeking confirmation if we seek the advice of unscrupulous or worldly people. This is one of the ways that we neglect to "acknowledge God in all our ways" (Prov. 3:6).

For example, you may own or manage a particular business or organization and you want to gain prominence in your community. So you may invite some well-known or influential people to sit on your board of directors. In the course of your business dealings, it may be revealed that one of them is a womanizer, or a drunkard, or has participated in some immoral, unethical, or even illegal activity. To keep that person on your board merely because they have connections, or are well-known may not be honoring God, and it may lead you into trouble. You may become entangled in their wrong-doing. Your reputation may be ruined if people assume that you are guilty by association. Or you may take their unscrupulous and unbiblical advice and find yourself in a terrible mess.

There is a concept called "pitching your tent toward Sodom." In the book of Genesis we see where Abraham and Lot broke into two separate camps because their servants were quarrelling. The Bible says:

> And Lot lifted his eyes and saw all the plain of Jordan, that it was well watered everywhere (before the Lord destroyed Sodom and Gomorrah) like the garden of the Lord, like the land of Egypt as you go toward Zoar. Then Lot chose for himself all the plain of Jordan, and Lot journeyed east. And they separated from each other.
> —Genesis 13:10-11, NKJV

The King James Version says in verse 12: "Lot ... pitched his tent toward Sodom."

We see in Genesis 14 that eventually Lot and his family moved right into the city of Sodom. When God judged the city for its wickedness, Lot had to be rescued by angels, but tragically he lost his wife in the process.

In making decisions, we must guard ourselves against "pitching our tent toward Sodom." It is easy to be enticed by the riches of this world and to make compromises to our beliefs in order to attain that wealth. But there is always a price to be paid for these compromises. This is another reason to utilize the seven keys in making major life decisions.

Be careful of whom you bring into your inner circle, and from whom your receive counsel. Edwin Louise Cole taught that you imbibe the spirit of the person under which you place yourself. I have seen this to be true time-and-time again in life. We take on the characteristics of those we surround ourselves with—even if it is ever so subtly. Eventually, we act on those characteristics. That is why it is imperative to surround yourself with godly men and women of character.

Show me your friends and I will show you your character, the old saying goes.

It is also dangerous to surround yourself with so-called "yes" men and women—people who will only tell you what they think you want to hear. This is particularly dangerous for people with wealth, power, or fame. They have the means to make big plans and to do great things. The people on their advisory board or in their top management team might be tempted to say what they think the leader wants to hear to keep their comfortable positions of power and wealth. This perilous situation has confronted many great Christian leaders in ministry, business, politics, education, the military, media, and other positions of power.

Christians can also make the mistake of surrounding themselves with people who do not tell them the truth. I have seen numerous instances of "mutual deception" societies in which co-dependent people latch onto one another to maintain a state of denial about areas of weakness in their lives. Sadly, there have been numerous believers who have come to ruin because they would not allow the people close to them to "speak the truth in love" to help them see clearly areas of weakness and even sin in their lives (see Eph. 4:15).

On the other hand, if God has spoken to you, and you know it is His voice beyond a shadow of a doubt, even if you receive contrary counsel from everybody else, it is wise to do what God says. Be sure to consider all the keys and ask the Lord to confirm His word to you with two or more witnesses before you act on that guidance. If you have done all these things and are confident in God's direction then move forward.

There are times when God will blind the eyes of those around you concerning His will in your life to test you to see if you are really following Him, or are unduly dependent on your mentors, family, and friends. That's not an easy place to be. When I left a particular evangelistic music ministry there were many around me who counseled me not to do it (though others counseled me to follow God's leading). But I knew beyond a shadow of a doubt that it was God's will for me and obeying Him was more important to me than pleasing my family and friends. God has blessed that decision, though for a time it caused a strain in some of those relationships.

If they are truly godly friends and counselors they will come back into fellowship with you in time, even if you don't follow their advice. Conversely, the person who breaks off their relationship with you because you don't follow their advice was never truly a friend to begin with.

Signs and Fleeces

There are times when God may confirm His direction to us through a specific sign—which is a biblical form of guidance from the Lord. Often He will do this because He wants us to see something in a clear way, or do something specific for Him. In these times He makes His way particularly clear, as He will require specific obedience from us. But it's important to point out that Jesus rebuked the Scribes and Pharisees, and even Thomas, when they sought a sign for confirmation in their unbelief. It's much better to have faith in God's ability to confirm His word to us in the way that He wants, rather than asking for some specific sign. If He wants to give us a sign, He is well able to do so in His sovereign and mighty power. But we should avoid waiting to move on a particular piece of guidance if we don't have a spectacular sign.

We may take something that is merely a coincidence as a sign and make a bad decision. Those kinds of decisions can take us off course and cost us dearly in time, money, and energy.

Another reason that signs can be dangerous is that they can be manufactured by Satan to get us off course. The Devil can come disguised as an angel of light (2 Cor. 11:14), and false signs may be sent to confuse us in our major decisions (2 Thes. 2:9). As an example, Moses and Aaron performed signs in front of Pharaoh to confirm that they were sent from God. Immediately, Pharaoh ordered his diviners to duplicate these signs with false miracles, and they did so (Ex. 7:10-11).

Jesus Himself warned of false prophets with false signs:

> Then if anyone says to you, 'Look, here is the Christ!' or 'There!' do not believe it. For false christs and false prophets will rise and show great signs and wonders to deceive, if possible, even the elect. See, I have told you beforehand. Therefore if they say to you, 'Look, He is in the desert!' do not go out; or 'Look, He is in the inner rooms!' do not believe it.
>
> —Matthew 24:23-26, NKJV

Jesus warned that many will be deceived by the Devil's lies because they will not have known the truth of God's Word. False miracles and false prophecies can lead us away from God's will. The seven keys we are studying in this book can help us to discern between the voice of God and the voice of the Devil—between a true sign from God and a counterfeit from the enemy.

There is also a difference between confirmation and the practice known as "fleecing"—something Gideon did to seek direction in the Old Testament. Someone might seek confirmation by setting out a fleece before God by saying, "If there is a rainbow in front of my house tomorrow then I will know that you want me to do such and such a thing." The danger in this approach to seeking confirmation is that it places too much emphasis on you telling God how He should or shouldn't confirm His will in your life. It's much safer to humbly allow God to determine how He will confirm His direction for us.

The other potential danger with setting out a fleece before the Lord lies once again in the realm of coincidence. What if you happened to say to God, "I want to see a rainbow in front of my house as a sign that I should marry this person." Then it just happens to rain because of the atmospheric conditions in your city the next day, so there just happens to be a rainbow that appears. I hope you understand what I am saying here. It was going to rain that day regardless of your prayer. The weather patterns were such that rainfall naturally occurred, and then the sun shone through the humid atmosphere and a rainbow appeared, just like it does every other time these events take place in this natural world. It was merely a coincidence that a rainbow appeared just after you prayed.

Fleecing has been a popular way of seeking God's guidance in some parts of the Church, but it should be noted that we only see one occurrence of fleecing as a method of seeking direction from the Lord in the Bible. When you carefully read Gideon's story you will see that he used the fleece because of his lack of faith in the word of the Lord— not exactly the best method for receiving guidance from heaven. In my opinion, fleecing is not a New Testament method of seeking guidance. In the story of Gideon, God accommodated his unbelief by answering his prayer for guidance through the fleece.

Today, we have the Bible and we have the Holy Spirit available on the inside of us to show us which direction to go—a tremendous blessing that Gideon did not have.

It's dangerous to make any decision based solely on fleeces and signs, which can be easily misinterpreted. I'm not saying that God does not give us signs to help guide us on our way—He absolutely does. But any sign should be weighed against the other keys of God's guidance, and it's best to allow God to choose what way He is going to confirm

His direction in your life, rather than trying to make that determination for Him.

Learning through Our Mistakes—and the Mistakes of Others

I have learned much from my father and am deeply in his debt for the wisdom he has shared with me over the years. One simple thing he told me when I was still an adolescent was, "Learn from the mistakes of others. You don't have time in life to make them all yourself."

We can learn from others mistakes, but also from their triumphs. The best situation would be if you could learn from someone else's mistakes without having to repeat them yourself. Try to reap as much wisdom as you can from as many individuals as you can. There is no one with a monopoly on wisdom. There are people who go through things in their life that we will never experience. We can gain the wisdom of their experience if we are willing to humble ourselves, listen, and learn from them.

We must also ask the Lord to help us learn from our own mistakes as well. In fact, we often learn as much or more about the will of God in making mistakes as we can learn in our triumphs. God can reinforce through negative circumstances in life as much as he can through the positive things that happen to us if we are humble and sensitive to His teaching. But we must step out of our comfort zone and be willing to make some mistakes in order to grow in our ability to hear God's voice.

God Wants to Confirm His Direction in Your Life

As we have established in this study, we absolutely can be led by the Holy Spirit and learn to know His will. Don't be afraid to ask God to confirm His plan for your life. He will not be offended by that request. It's better to wait until you are at peace with the leading of the Lord than to rush out ahead of God and possibly miss His timing.

God wants to lead us. He wants to reveal His will to us through many different means—the Bible; the voice of the Lord speaking to your heart; personal prophecy; godly counsel; peace; circumstances; visions; dreams; angelic visitations; various signs—all of these things can be used by God to confirm His will for your life. God can speak to you in one of a million ways. He is God, and He can reveal Himself to you any way He wants to—and the greatest thing is that He does want to!

Questions For Meditation

1. Why might your own desire be an important factor to consider when seeking God's guidance?

2. Read Acts 2:17-18. What does this passage tell us about the gifts of the Holy Spirit in our day?

   "In the last days," God says, "I will pour out my Spirit upon all people. Your sons and daughters will prophesy. Your young men will see visions, and your old men will dream dreams. In those days I will pour out my Spirit even on my servants—men and women alike—and they will prophesy."

—Acts 2:17-18, NLT

3. Write down a list of all the different ways that God directed his people in the Bible.

4. Now write down all the ways you have been led by the spirit of God in your lifetime.

5. From what you've learned so far in this Bible study, what are some of the ways that God leads that you have not yet experienced, but that you may extend your faith to believe for in the future?

6. How does the promise, "when you ask for the Holy Spirit, you're going to get the Holy Spirit," bring peace to you as you seek God's direction for your life?

7. Have you ever experienced a "divine rejection"? If so, what were the circumstances? What was the end result?

8. Describe a time in your life when you asked God for something, and he did not give it to you at that time, but later he gave you something even better. What did you learn from this experience?

9. Have you ever had to die to a vision? What was the end result of surrendering it to the Lord?

10. How can you tell the difference between a true and the false friend when it comes to seeking counsel?

11. What do you see as the primary dangers in setting out a fleece?

12. How can sin and unforgiveness keep you from hearing God's voice?

Chapter Eleven

Circumstances – Hearing God in Every Day Life

One of the strongest man-made structures in the world is a suspension bridge. This modern engineering marvel can carry an amazing amount of weight and strain because of its unique design. Every suspension bridge includes at least two anchors at each end of the structure to bear the load. Then giant steel cables are strung back and forth from one anchor to the other. The actual roadway is suspended in mid-air from these enormous cables. If there were a failure in one or the other anchor the entire structure would collapse. That's why the towers that support a suspension bridge need to be massive, incredibly strong, and anchored in bedrock.

Not only is it a practical part of our modern transportation system, the suspension bridge is also a thing of beauty. Some of the world's great man-made structures include suspension bridges like the Golden Gate and the Brooklyn Bridge.

A proper biblical worldview sometimes demands that we approach God's truth by weighing the Scriptures and opinions on both ends of an issue and then coming to a balanced position in the middle—like the roadway on a suspension bridge. I call this philosophy "truths in tension," and we see numerous occasions where it is demonstrated throughout the Bible. For example, there are many scriptures that admonish the community of believers to take care of the poor. But the Bible also says if you don't work, you don't eat. The truth of how to respond to the poor among us is somewhere balanced between these two concepts.

When considering how God uses circumstances to guide us, we should look at the balance of two truths; first, God can and does use circumstances to guide us into His will; and second, circumstances are not always an indication of God's plan for our lives.

It's probably easier to be swayed by circumstances than by any of the other keys to God's guidance because circumstances are so real to us in the physical world. Anything that touches our person in this world is circumstance—joy, sorrow, hunger, pain, happiness, cold, heat, birth, and death.

When it comes to being led through circumstances it seems that many Christians are clinging to one or the other end of the suspension bridge. Some are convinced that the manifestation of the Holy Spirit, along with God's willingness to speak to His children, ended with the death of the last early Church apostle. These folks are hanging onto the anchor that God only leads through the Bible and circumstances. Then there are those who are on the other end of the bridge, believing that God leads only through supernatural signs and not at all through circumstances.

I believe the truth is in the balance of both extremes. As we have already seen in our study, God does lead His children in many different ways. But He will also use the circumstances of our lives to direct us into His will. Many so-called "hyper-spiritual" believers have walked right out of God's will because they didn't want to be bothered by the circumstances of life. The ramifications of this spiritual arrogance can lead to major catastrophes.

Other so-called "grounded evangelicals" have ignored the voice of the Lord speaking to their heart or a supernatural sign He has placed in their path and have focused only on the circumstances that they perceive with their natural senses. These folks are often either extremely limited in their impact for the kingdom of God, or they are completely blind to spiritual matters. They are like the perilous person described as "having a form of godliness, but denying its power," whom Paul warned against in 2 Timothy 3:5. The truth is that you are a spirit, you have a soul, and you live in a body. God can and will communicate with all aspects of who you are. He will use every means necessary to reach you with His message of love and grace.

Remember, God is love—and love communicates—through any means He chooses.

Open and Closed Doors

Abraham Lincoln is an amazing example of person who, despite hindering circumstances, pushed forward in life until he achieved his divine destiny. He was born into poverty and as a youngster, Lincoln had to work to help support the family. He received almost no reward for his grueling labor, as it all went toward the needs of the family. In 1818 his mother died, which brought great sorrow to young Abraham. Later, in 1835 he was engaged to be married, but his sweetheart also died unexpectedly, leaving him in a state of depression.

After losing one of two elections for the United States Senate, he proclaimed the optimistic outlook that kept him moving forward despite all the setbacks. On the walk home in the rain, after learning of his defeat, he slipped on a muddy hill and almost fell. He later wrote of the experience:

> The path was worn and slippery. My foot slipped from under me, knocking the other out of the way, but I recovered and said to myself, "It is a slip and not a fall."[40]

Though he lost the election, his rousing debates with his opponent, Stephen Douglas, brought him to the attention of the entire nation—especially due to his eloquent opposition to slavery.

Two years later, the resilient Abraham Lincoln was elected President of the United States. He would go on to save

---

[40] Fehrenbacher, Don and Virginia. *Recollected Words of Abraham Lincoln.* (Stanford: Stanford University Press. 1996) 232.

the Union and free the slaves, becoming one of the greatest of American presidents.

Lincoln is a member of a distinguished group of winners who didn't believe it when people said they were losers:

- After Fred Astaire's first screen test, the memo from the testing director of MGM, dated 1933, said, *Can't act! Slightly bald! Can dance a little!* Astaire kept that memo over the fireplace in his Beverly Hills home.

- An "expert" said of American football coach Vince Lombardi: "He possesses minimal football knowledge. Lacks motivation."

- Beethoven handled the violin awkwardly and preferred playing his own compositions instead of improving his technique. His teacher called him hopeless as a composer.

- Walt Disney was fired by a newspaper editor for lack of ideas. Disney also went bankrupt before he built Disneyland.

- Albert Einstein did not speak until he was four years old and didn't read until he was seven. His teacher described him as "mentally slow, unsociable and adrift forever in his foolish dreams." He was expelled and was refused admittance to the Zurich Polytechnic School.

- Louis Pasteur was only a mediocre pupil in undergraduate studies and ranked 15th out of 22 classmates in chemistry.

- Leo Tolstoy, author of *War and Peace,* flunked out of college. He was described as "both unable and unwilling to learn."

- Babe Ruth, considered by sports historians to be one of the greatest baseball players of all time and famous for setting the home run record, also holds the record for strikeouts.

- Winston Churchill failed sixth grade. He did not become Prime Minister of England until he was 62, and then only after a lifetime of defeats and setbacks. His greatest contributions came when he was a "senior citizen."

God will often use what man would call "closed doors" to mold our character and prepare us for the pre-ordained time when we fulfill His destiny for our lives. In *My Utmost for His Highest,* Oswald Chambers explained that not everything that happens to us as Christians makes human sense.

> To turn head faith into a personal possession is a fight always, not sometimes. God brings us into circumstances in order to exercise our faith.[41]

Maturity comes to believers when they allow the Holy Spirit to break them of their vulnerability to circumstances in life. One of my favorite teachers, Larry Tomczak, said,

> You're not under the circumstances, you're above the circumstances. You don't contend with the Devil for a place

---

[41] Chambers, Oswald. *My Utmost for His Highest.* Online: articles.ochristian.com/article10057.shtml

of victory, you overcome him from your position of victory."[42]

Circumstances taken as the leading of the Holy Spirit, apart from consideration of the Scriptures and the peace of God, can lead us astray. We must learn to discern God's hand in both positive and negative circumstances. But neither favorable nor unfavorable circumstances can be taken alone as a sign that we are in or out of the will of God.

There are two types of circumstances that God will use to lead us—closed doors and open doors.

Closed doors restrain us from moving forward in our pursuits. This can be frustrating at times, and when it happens it should force us to seek the Lord as to why the door appears to be closed, especially if it seems that we have had clear guidance to move in that direction. Some Christians automatically think that a closed door is Satan's attempt to prevent God's plan from happening in their lives. Others believe the closed door is a sign that God is saying no to that pursuit. Both of these extremes can be dangerous, because they may be right, or they may be wrong. One needs spiritual discernment to discover God's purpose in the closed doors of life—and that can be found in using all of the 7 keys to God's guidance.

We often interpret the negative circumstances of life in one of four ways:

---

[42] Tomczak, Larry. *Biblical Confessions to Increase Your Faith,* audio cassette, 1998.

1. God is putting me through a test;
2. I'm reaping the wages of my sin;
3. I'm being attacked by the Devil; or
4. I'm being persecuted for righteousness' sake.

Any of these statements could be the true diagnosis of the situation. But it takes more than an analysis of circumstances to know for sure. Just because a door is closed doesn't mean it will be closed forever. Sometimes the Lord places us in a holding pattern while He works on our character, or while He is setting the stage for our later success. The Bible and history show us innumerable instances of people persevering through difficulties and delays along the path to their destiny.

God can also lead us through the seemingly open doors that circumstances present. These potential open doors can be exciting and can seem like a clear indication of God's will for our lives. But one must beware. Not every open door is from God.

Blaine Smith classifies open doors into two categories—suggestive or confirming:

> Suggestive circumstances imply possibilities. Receiving a scholarship would suggest the possibility of attending a particular college. But this circumstance should align with the other guidance factors of desire, ability, and counsel. Confirming circumstances merely confirm the choice, which we believe to be God's will. If you have already

determined that you are to marry a particular person, then circumstances may simply confirm your decision.[43]

When things don't seem to be working out, or you're having a difficult time with the circumstances of your life, it isn't always because you're out of the plan of God. Often you are directly in His will. Circumstances can help you determine the will of God, but they should never be an ultimate indication of it. It's important to take everything you are hearing from God into account—and use all 7 keys to evaluate the message.

Our days are preordained by God. King David wrote in Psalm 139:16,

> Your eyes saw my substance, being yet unformed. And in Your book they all were written, the days fashioned for me, when as yet there were none of them.
>
> —Psalm 139:16

We can rejoice in knowing that the sovereign God has things well in hand. When we sense a witness in our spirit, then we can to look for the circumstances to line up, confirming that it is indeed the will of God.

The Fire of Delayed Answers

Waiting for God's timing is a critical element of being led by the Spirit. Circumstances can help us to gage the timing of the Lord, which is often like a traffic light. There is the red light of stop, the yellow light of caution, or "slow down," and

---

[43] Smith, M. Blaine, *Guidance by the Book*, © 1992, CBN Publishing, Virginia Beach, VA.

the green light of go. We may have God's direction on a matter, but the circumstances don't line up—the light of God's timing is red. Other times we know God's will, and it seems like things are coming together, but we still wait for certain key issues to fall into place—the light of God's timing is yellow. But when you know God's will, all the circumstances have fallen into place, and you have peace in your heart, the light is green—it's time to move forward.

In his book, *When God Winks*, Squire Rushnell explains how God will lead us through life's circumstances:

> A God Wink is ... a message of reassurance coming when you most need it: when you're at a crossroads in your life, and when instability is all around. It might be said, in fact, that coincidences are the best way for God to establish a perpetual presence in your life. Think about it. If you were God and wanted to communicate with human beings without using a human voice, how would you do it? You'd perform little miracles, wouldn't you? ...coincidences, that cause people to say, 'What are the odds of this ever happening?' Those are God Winks.[44]

Isn't that a wonderful way of describing how God is constantly at work, leading us into His perfect will for our lives?

Circumstances can be a factor in the leading of God in your life, but you don't want your life to be controlled merely by circumstances. Through God's power and sovereignty seemingly negative circumstances can change.

---

[44] Rushnell, SQuire, *When God Winks*, © 2001, Atria Books.

Circumstances should be considered, but they are not to be a final factor in making decisions for our lives.

Sometimes the answer to our difficult circumstances seems to be delayed—but this is another way God may use to direct our steps.

There may be times where the Lord will allow you to go through certain things that don't seem to make sense. It may seem that He is not answering your prayers, or that the Devil has been given a free pass to harass you. Your whole world may seem like it's crumbling around you—and that may even be true. The Lord may be allowing you to be tested for a season to show you your own heart and to help you to grow in godly character.

James writes famously of this phenomenon in the Christian experience:

> Dear brothers and sisters, when troubles of any kind come your way, consider it an opportunity for great joy. For you know that when your faith is tested, your endurance has a chance to grow. So let it grow, for when your endurance is fully developed, you will be perfect and complete, needing nothing.
> —James 1:2-4, NLT

God will deliver us from affliction, but sometimes He will delay the answer for the purpose of refining us by fire. In this life we are in the process of growing into maturity in Christ. The Lord wants to produce His character in us so that we can be an example of His love and grace to this lost and dying world. Sometimes the only way that God can work on these deep-seated areas is by allowing us to go through the fires of adversity.

God wants His first commandment—to love the Lord your God—to be the first priority in our lives, and the second commandment—to love others—to be the second. He uses the fiery circumstances of life's tests and trials to bring us to a deeper love for Himself, and from that love flows our desire to minister to others.

If you have done all you need to do to receive God's direction but the answer has not yet come, then stand firm in faith, trusting that the Lord will bring it about in His good time. God is good, all the time! He delights in blessing His children—but He also delights in seeing His children mature into the men and women that He desires for them to be.

The Harness of the Holy Spirit

Horses are some of the most beautiful and powerful of God's creatures. Left to run wild, a horse is a ferocious and potentially dangerous creature. But once it is trained—and under the bit and bridle of its master—a horse can perform amazing feats of strength and skill, and is one of the most graceful creatures on earth.

You and I are a lot like that, aren't we? We need God to temper us and to lead us. As the 23rd Psalm says:

> He leads me beside quiet waters.
> —Psalm 23:2, NASB

Without His leading how lost we would be?

It's especially important to have God's leading when we go through difficult times. In the dark days we must strive to be "tuned in" to the voice of the Lord.

The Lord showed me an illustration of this during a difficult transition in my life when He called me out of the ministry for a time.

For nearly five years I had traveled with a Christian rock band called *Insight*. The Lord had blessed us as thousands of young people committed their lives to Christ through our ministry. But then the Lord began to show me in my time of prayer that I had completed the work He wanted me to do with the band and He had other plans for my life.

I felt like Abraham when the Lord called him out of Ur of the Chaldees. The Lord promised to lead me, but He didn't tell me where I was going.

It was difficult for many people in my life to understand why the Lord would take me out of a fruit-bearing field and put me into the wilderness. But as I read the Bible I discovered that this is His pattern for training leaders. Jesus was tempted in the desert. Paul, Moses, John the Baptist, King David and others spent years in the wilderness learning to hear and trust God. If I were to be a servant of Jesus Christ, I would have my desert experiences as well.

I spent a grueling year seeking the Lord's direction for my life. During this time I worked a construction job, renovating a Victorian house. While I enjoyed working with my hands, doing manual labor as a full-time job was not what I felt called to as an occupation. Looking back now however, I can see the good things that God did in my heart during that dry time.

One day as I worked in the hot, dirty attic of a 100-year-old home I cried out to the Lord. "God, have you brought me out to the desert to kill me? I left college after three years to manage the ministry. Now you tell me to leave the band but you don't tell me where to go."

Suddenly I saw a picture in my spirit. The Lord reminded me of the days when I would go horseback riding with my friends in college. We would ride over the grassy hills of the Allegheny Mountains, feeling the exhilaration of that mighty creature moving at our command. God designed horses to run. A horse would run all the time if it could. What a wonderful thing it was to experience a part of the joy that this majestic animal felt as he galloped over the rolling hills.

The Lord reminded me of how we used to take the horses into the woods. "Be careful," my experienced friend would caution. "Hold very tightly to the reins as we pass through the trees. There are fallen logs and moss-covered rocks that the horse could slip on if you don't take it slow." If a horse is injured in the woods it's almost impossible to save it from destruction.

I remembered how my arms would become strained pulling back on the reins, trying to keep that beautiful beast from going any faster than a slow walk. The struggle became much more intense as we approached the edge of the forest. The horses sensed the clearing was near and it became increasingly difficult to keep them from running. It took all of my might to hold those reins tight.

When we finally emerged onto the meadow, without any prodding at all the horses took off in a full speed gallop.

"You are like that horse," the Lord spoke gently to my heart. "I designed you with My power to run. Right now, however, you are going through a season where I am guiding you through the woods. I'm holding tight to your reins so you won't slip on a moss-covered rock or trip over a fallen log."

The Master knew the destination of my life. He knew that soon I too would emerge onto that spiritual meadow where I would be allowed to run free in the calling He had for me. The Devil would have liked nothing more than to see me stumble and fall in the woods. He loves to see us run out ahead of God's timing and fall under the weight of our own zeal. There are those who have fallen in the woods that the enemy has tried to utterly destroy.

"For now my child," the Father said gently, "rest and allow Me to guide you through this delicate time. Do not resist My direction but flow with it and you will be safe."

Hearing God's voice is especially critical in times of emotional upheaval, temptation, or when making a big decision—this is when we are symbolically walking through the woods. The good news is that:

> He guides the humble in what is right and teaches them His way.
> —Psalm 25:9, NIV

There have been times of discouragement in that season and since, but the illustration of the harness of the Holy Spirit has come back to comfort me again and again as I follow the Lord.

Staying the Course

There may come a time when you receive guidance from Lord that you believe is beyond the shadow of a doubt—and the other keys of God's guidance confirm it—so you proceed in faith, but suddenly you find yourself facing all sorts of opposition to the very thing God called you to do. You may wonder why God is not protecting you from the attacks of the enemy. After all, you are doing what He commissioned you to do.

If this is occurring, don't be dismayed—this scenario is common in the Christian life. Jesus promised persecution to those who would follow Him. But He also promised His grace to help us through the difficult times. When guidance is clearly given by the Lord, confirmed by witnesses, and established in your heart, you can bet the Devil will do what he can to get you off track in the form of persecution and adverse circumstances. At those times you must set your face like flint to do that which the Lord has clearly revealed, no matter what is happening around you to take you off course.

When you have the clear word of the Lord, with no ambiguity, there is no reason to fear when the circumstances turn sour. In fact, you can almost expect it to happen.

We are constantly navigating a labyrinth of contrasting circumstances in life. A mature Christian will not merely react to what he or she senses in the natural world, but they will consistently inquire of the Lord to give discernment on how to interpret the circumstance they are facing.

Sometimes difficult circumstances are the result of our own past mistakes—even before we were Christians. The Lord can redeem the tragedies and mistakes of our past, even when they are completely our fault. In fact, this is one of the ways that God makes Himself real to other people in our lives. When our family, friends, and acquaintances see how

God has moved dramatically to change your character and your circumstances, they have to ask how it all happened. My Dad's motto is, "Every blessing becomes a burden, and every burden has its blessings." God will do a Romans 8:28 transformation for "those who are called according to His purpose." This wonderful transformation in life gives us the opportunity to tell others of the newfound freedom that comes through a relationship with Jesus Christ!

The Shepherd of Our Circumstances

Big decisions in life are often stressful—who to marry, what job to take, what house to buy, where to go to college, whether or not to start a business—the pressures of life can sometimes bring great anxiety. When faced with such decisions it's often difficult to hear the Lord's voice. Our emotions can be very loud. In these times, it's vitally important to prayerfully consider all the seven keys of God's guidance.

The Lord is familiar with the frailty of mankind and in His mercy He will often use circumstances as signposts to point us toward His will when we are at an important crossroads. If you believe God is speaking to you through circumstances, pray that He will confirm His direction through one or more of the other keys. Remember, that direction must line up with the Word of God, and if it truly is of the Lord it will be accompanied by God's peace.

God has the power to ordain the circumstances in your life to direct you toward His will. He can cause negative circumstances to show that you are veering away from His plan for your life. Be aware when the little annoyances start building around you—personality conflicts at work or home when it is normally peaceful, a series of things breaking down in your car or in your house—if the peace of your existence is upset for an extended period of time it may be that God is trying to get your attention.

One of my pastors often spoke about the umbrella of God's protection. When you are walking in right relationship with God, listening for His voice, and then obeying His commands, the Lord provides this umbrella that shields you from the storm. Now there are times when the Lord allows things to get through this shield of faith to test our character. There are other times when the Devil will bring an attack. But for the most part the Lord keeps and protects His sheep from the wolves on the outside, and from their own foolishness inside the pen. Then from time to time a shepherd will nudge the sheep with his staff to get them to move forward, or to keep them from danger. Thank God that He uses the rod of circumstances to nudge us into His will or away from things that will harm us.

If we are truly surrendered to God, praying for His will to be done, He will bring His good pleasure to pass. If God wants you to have a certain house, He will give you the means to buy it, the right price to offer, and sellers who are favorable to you and your family. If God wants you to marry that person, He will put the desire in both of your hearts, and He will confirm it to both of you. If God wants you to move across the country to take that job, He will give you the peace that the move is of Him, and He will give you favor with your potential employer. If none of these things happen, rest assured that God still has an amazing plan for your life.

It's imperative that Christians seek with all their heart to be in the center of God's will (Matt. 6:33). God is pleased when His children desire to do what He wants us to do. It's a sign of our love for Him that we are willing to humble ourselves and say, "I want your plan more than I want my plan."

Bob Mumford tells the story of an evangelist who was driving across Florida with his family.

> His wife asked him to stop in a certain town to get some orange juice for the children. They just happened to turn off at a certain exit, drove down a block or two, and pulled up in front of a fruit-stand. Before he had time to get out of the car a lady came running across the street.
>
> "Are you a minister?" she asked breathlessly.
>
> "Yes," he replied.
>
> "Praise the Lord!" she exclaimed. "This morning I prayed that God would send a minister who would lay hands on me and pray for my healing. God said you'd be driving a station wagon and be pulling a trailer." She looked at the evangelist's brown station wagon and trailer and asked, "What took you so long?"
>
> Bob Mumford explains that this evangelist and his wife didn't know anything about God's plan for them that afternoon. They hadn't heard a voice saying, "Turn off at this exit and drive two blocks to the fruit-stand where there is a lady I want you to pray for." But they had committed their day to God and prayed before leaving that His will and plan for that day would come to pass. And so the circumstance of the children's thirst and need for vitamin C caused them to

move into the sovereign plan of God for them and for the woman who needed prayer.[45]

When we completely yield ourselves to God's plan, sincerely praying, "not my will, but your will be done," it's amazing how the Lord will orchestrate circumstances to move us toward His desire for our lives. We will often find ourselves in the right place at the right time for God's providence to work on our behalf.

You can take comfort that no matter what the circumstances God has a plan for your life, and He will guide your steps. He has given us His promise:

> Being confident of this, that he who began a good work in you will carry it on to completion until the day of Christ Jesus.
>
> —Phillipians 1:6, NIV

Questions For Meditation

1. What do you think Oswald Chambers meant when he said, "God brings us into circumstances in order to exercise our faith?"

2. Why do you think that some people are guided by circumstances alone, while others almost completely ignore circumstances when seeking God for decisions? Where is the balance for you?

3. How can you rightly discern if an open or closed door is from the Lord?

---

[45] Mumford, Bob, *Take Another Look at Guidance*, Plainfield, NJ: Logos Publishers, 1971.

4. Have you ever experienced a "God wink" in your life? What happened? How did you know it was from God?
5. When have you experienced the "harness of the Holy Spirit"?
6. Read Philippians 4:4–13. How does Paul respond to whatever circumstances in which he finds himself?

> Always be full of joy in the Lord. I say it again—rejoice! Let everyone see that you are considerate in all you do. Remember, the Lord is coming soon. Don't worry about anything; instead, pray about everything. Tell God what you need, and thank him for all he has done. Then you will experience God's peace, which exceeds anything we can understand. His peace will guard your hearts and minds as you live in Christ Jesus.
>
> And now, dear brothers and sisters, one final thing. Fix your thoughts on what is true, and honorable, and right, and pure, and lovely, and admirable. Think about things that are excellent and worthy of praise. Keep putting into practice all you learned and received from me—everything you heard from me and saw me doing. Then the God of peace will be with you.
>
> How I praise the Lord that you are concerned about me again. I know you have always been concerned for me, but you didn't have the chance to help me. Not that I was ever in need, for I have learned how to be content with whatever I have. I know how to live on almost nothing or with everything. I have learned the secret of living in every situation, whether it is with a full stomach or empty, with plenty or little. For I can do everything through Christ, who gives me strength.
>
> —Phillipians 4:4-13, NLT

7. When you are facing a stressful decision, how can your circumstances be a guidepost of God's direction?

8. At the same time, how might circumstances lead us away from God's plan? How can we tell the difference?

CHAPTER TWELVE

TRULY HEARING GOD – SEEKING THE MAKER OF THE STARS

In a recent Barna Research study, 68 percent of those surveyed, including 58 percent of non-Christians, and 83 percent of born-again Christians, said that they are facing a decision for which they "would like to get direction from God."[46] It's not surprising that both Christians and non-Christian gave this response. God wired us to seek Him.

As this study shows, guidance is a step-by-step walk with the Lord over the course of a lifetime. Hearing God's voice and being led by His Spirit comes down to recognizing our total dependence on the Lord. Without Him we are a ship

---

[46] Jeffress, Robert, *Hearing the Master's Voice*, © 2001, Waterbrook Press, Colorado Springs, CO.

adrift at sea. Jesus clearly painted the picture of our condition in this world when he told his disciples:

> I am the vine, you are the branches, He who abides in Me, and I in him, bears much fruit; for without Me you can do nothing.
>
> —John 15:5, NKJV

As disciples, we must never forget the most important thing of all is to "abide in the vine," to keep our relationship with our Creator, the Maker of the stars, and the most important priority in our lives.

Intimate Moments with the Savior

It was an issue of blood—but not blood only. You see the diabetes that wracked my friend Dick's body had also damaged his liver and destroyed his kidneys. But it was the issue of blood—the lack of circulation—that made Dick's trial most evident to the rest of us. This was especially true when he underwent surgery to amputate his leg as a result of diabetes.

Working together at the Christian Broadcasting Network, Dick and I had experienced the presence of God during times of prayer or worship. But when I heard that Dick had gone to be with the Lord, I was reminded of one particularly sweet moment we shared—it was an intimate moment with the Savior.

I was asked to lead chapel in our department during a telethon. As I prayed about what I was to share, I felt the

Lord directing me to read from a special devotional by Ken Gire called *Intimate Moments With The Savior*.[47]

Before the meeting began, I was told that Dick was facing yet another surgery. He had already had some of his toes removed and it appeared that the doctors were going to have to amputate even more from his foot. The diabetes was cutting off circulation and if they didn't act, gangrene would set in.

My heart was heavy as I led our time of prayer, and I could see the weight that Dick was carrying on his shoulders. I opened the devotional to where we had left off the day before. Providentially, that day we would read about the woman with the issue of blood from Mark 5:24-34. After writing out the Scripture passage, Gire writes his interpretation of the events:

> God only knows how much she's suffered. She has lived with a bleeding uterus for twelve humiliating years. She has been labeled unclean by the rabbis and subjected to the Levitical prohibitions "Orphaned by society." And orphaned also by God, or so she thinks. She has prayed. She has pleaded. But for twelve agonizing years God has been silent.
>
> She is destitute now. And being out of money, the doctors finally admit there is nothing they can do for her. Her life is ebbing away. The steady loss of blood over the years has taken its toll. She is anemic, pale, and tired. So very, very tired.

As I read these words, a wave of emotion washed over me. I looked across the table and Dick was stooped over, like an

---

[47] Gire, Ken, *Intimate Moments with the Savior*. (Grand Rapids: Zondervan Publishing, 1989) 47-50.

old man carrying a pack that he could barely lift. His eyes were tightly shut, and he was drinking in the details of this sad story. I continued to read:

> She no longer dreams of marriage and a family—of being taken care of in her old age by loved ones—of golden memories she can treasure. Her suffering has whisked those dreams into little broken piles.
>
> But stories of another physician reach down to pick up the pieces of those dreams. A physician who charges no fee. A physician who asks nothing in return. Who has no hidden agenda beyond making a sick world well again.
>
> She has heard of this physician, this Jesus who comes not to the healthy but to the sick. Who comes not to the strong but to the downtrodden. Who comes not to those with well-ordered lives but to those whose lives are filled with physical and moral chaos.
>
> "She has heard of Jesus' success among incurables— "Certainly," she thinks, "if I can find this Jesus and but touch the fringe of his garment, I too will be cleansed and made whole."

As I conveyed the story, a strange mixture of emotions swept through me. It was as if I could see into the future to experience the struggles that would confront my friend. I was overcome with sadness and I began to weep.

But the words I read aloud about the love and compassion shown by Jesus to this woman mixed into my sadness a comforting feeling of hope and peace. As I continued, I was suddenly confident that the same loving care that Jesus showed to this woman two thousand years ago would be shown to my friend.

> This desperate woman pushes her empty hand through a broken seam in the crowd and, for a fleeting moment, clutches the corner of his garment. Jesus is pulled back. Not by the grasp of her hands so much as by the grasp of her faith. Power leaves him to surge through the hemorrhaging woman, and immediately she feels the rush of her youthful health returning—How ready Jesus is to respond to the hand of outstretched faith.

I was overcome with the revelation of God's grace and His kindness—again the tears flowed down my cheeks, and I had to stop reading. I glanced through my clouded eyes at Dick. He, too, had tears, but they were just small pools collected in the corners of his eyes. Dick and his family had cried many tears as they faced the same indignities and humiliations as the woman in the story—he may not have had any more tears to cry.

But if his ongoing ordeal had made him bitter, he never let us know.

As a matter of fact, Dick was one of the most joyful Christians I knew. He always smiled when we greeted each other in the hall. He was an encourager, giving other employees a word of praise for a job well done. And he was always there when it was time to pray; he knew that the intimate moments with the Savior were what sustained him.

The presence of the Lord was so strong in our little gathering on that day, and I knew God was doing something special. When I finished reading, I asked the others to join me in praying for Dick. We gathered around and laid our hands on this dear man. You could sense him drawing strength from the words of faith being lifted up to heaven on his behalf. When we finished, many were wiping tears from their eyes.

As we rose to leave, Dick asked to borrow my devotional. "I have a feeling I'm going to need to experience more of these intimate moments with the Savior," he declared.

He told me later that he read through the small book several times. He needed to know God's presence in the weeks and months that followed as the doctors amputated most of Dick's foot, and then his leg below the knee.

Dick returned to work in a wheel chair. As the year progressed his body slowly succumbed to the disease. His kidneys failed and he was placed on the donor list for a liver transplant. But through it all, Dick continued to find strength in the Savior. He made it to work as often as he could, and his work for the Lord at CBN was stellar.

He had recently been reassigned to a new project in a different department. On his last day of work in our department, which was a Friday, he finished all of his tasks, cleared his desk, and handed the books to his supervisor. His co-workers gathered around to pray for him and send him off to his new role with a blessing.

Little did they know.

On the final day of his life, Dick took his family to church. After the service, his wife and kids treated him to his favorite restaurant for lunch. Later that evening, as Dick worked at his dining room table, he was given his new assignment—and his new home.

You see, it was an issue of blood. Dick had surrendered his life to God. The shed blood of Jesus that purchased Dick's redemption was the life force that sustained him when his own circulation began to fail.

God only knows how much Dick suffered over the years, just like the woman with the issue of blood. Ken Gire finishes the story:

> The crowd blurs in the watery edges of her eyes. For an intimate moment she sees only Jesus. And he sees only her. Face to face, physician and patient. And with the tender word "Daughter," he gives this orphan a new home within the family of God. He gives her healing. And he gives her back her dreams.[48]

For my friend Dick, in an intimate moment, God gave him back his dreams—and a new, glorified body. Dick's walk with God through the years of pain was an issue of faith. His joy in the midst of the trial was an issue of praise. And his new assignment in the presence of his Lord and Savior was an issue of blood.

I share this story of my dear friend to encourage you as you seek to hear the voice of God in your relationship with him. This life is filled with the struggles that we all face—some are physical, like what my friend Dick faced. Some of us deal with challenges in our marriages and families. You may be facing financial hardships. Others battle with emotional difficulties, like depression or anxiety. Then there are those who face the more subtle obstacles in life. Things on the outside seem to be going great, but inside, you may struggle with pride, anger, lust, or a controlling spirit.

---

[48]Gire, Ken, *Intimate Moments with the Savior*, Grand Rapids, MI: Zondervan Publishing House, pp. 47-50.

Whatever our challenges, we all have issues that can potentially hinder us in our relationship with God.

The Lord wants to communicate with us, and he is constantly sending His messages. As much as we desire to be a receiver, there is the constant distraction of "noise." In this modern world the "noise" is both external and internal. This "noise" can be psychological, emotional, spiritual, and even physical. There will always be something that will potentially distract us from hearing God.

We live in a loud world. There are people I know who can't go a minute of their day—including their sleeping hours—without some sort of sound. If it's not the television, it's the radio, music player, or Internet—anything to keep them from being quiet. Some of these people are hurting so much they don't want to face the world inside—and they definitely don't want to hear God's voice.

Then there are the people who live loud—they are on the move, in charge, the alpha-male types, with the cell phone in their hand night and day. They go from the power breakfast with the partners in the company, to the power lunch with the key client, to the elegant dinner with the beautiful woman or handsome man. They don't see their need to hear the voice of God.

And then there is the person like my friend Dick, who truly loves the Lord, and wants to find His plan for their life. They want to do the best job for God and his or her family as possible. But like Dick, the challenges of living in this fallen world can constantly distract from the walk with God that you desire.

I suspect this description may fit you as you are reading these words. You wouldn't have gotten this far in this book if you didn't truly want to learn to hear God's voice and follow His direction for your life. I want to encourage you—you are on the right track. That's how Dick lived his life. It didn't matter what challenges he faced in his physical body, or in his emotional reaction to the obstacles that came against him, he continued to press forward in God.

We see a symbol of this struggle in the Old Testament Passover meal as the Children of Israel ate the bitter herbs, but they also enjoyed the sweet meat of the Lamb. It's the same in our walk with the Lord today. Like Dick, we all experience the bitterness of life's difficulties. But as Dick so gracefully displayed in his life of joyful, diligent service to the Lord, we can also enjoy the sweet meat that comes from a daily relationship with the Lamb of God.

Dick understood that hearing God's voice and walking in His blessings is all about relationship. No matter what you face in life, or how loud the noise gets, find a place where you can go to be alone with God and listen for His voice—because that intimate time with the Savior—abiding in the vine—is the wellspring of life.

Finally Making a Decision

After all of the seven keys have been considered the time will finally come to make the actual decision—but even then, it is still imperative to be sensitive to God's voice.

If we have surrendered our lives to the lordship of Jesus Christ and made things right in a spiritual sense, it's time to practically consider the decision we are making. We have examined the options in light of the seven keys: the Scripture; what the Holy Spirit has revealed to our heart; godly counsel; the peace of God; personal prophecy; confirmation; and circumstances. Before making a final decision, we need to carefully examine the entire situation using our God-given intellect. Ask yourself these questions:

- Is this new direction Biblical?

- Is my spouse in agreement with this decision?

- Does this complement my spiritual gifts?

- Can I use my God-given talents and abilities in this new role?

- Does this new direction line up with the long-term desires of my heart?

- Do I have the personal resources to move forward in this direction?

- Will I have to wait on God's timing to bring those resources to me or to my organization?

- Do I have the experience necessary to excel in this new area of responsibility? Or, is God asking me to go out and gain the experience needed to move into this new venture?

- Is it ethical? Is it legal? Is it moral?

- Do I have the peace of Christ—not necessarily a complete and total freedom from concern—but do I have enough assurance from the Lord that He will guide me in this new path?

- Will my decision fulfill a desire that has been planted in my heart?
- What are key people around me saying about this new direction—parents, pastors, professors, mentors, and friends? How has my decision been balanced on the scales of their opinions?
- Are the circumstantial doors opened or are they closed?
- If the doors seem to be closed does that mean I should back away, or do I have enough assurance through the other keys to wait in faith for God to bring the circumstances in line?
- If the doors seem to be open, do I have enough assurance that God has spoken through the other keys for me to move forward in this decision?
- Am I willing to die to my own desires if the Lord directs me in a way that I did not expect, or that I have been opposed to in the past?
- Am I willing to allow God to give me the desire of my heart, even though it means new, and possibly frightening challenges—and even a loss of my comfort zone?

After considering this list of questions, you are ready to move forward in your decision. Once you are confident you know God's will and have His peace, take that step of faith and watch what God will do. Just like He did with Peter, when you lift your foot over the edge of the boat and step onto the water in obedience to His call, grace will come on the scene and God will do what it takes to see His will accomplished in your life.

As you make your decision, remember that second thoughts are normal. Everyone experiences doubts, fears, and uneasiness during a major transition in life. Trust the Lord every step of the way. Go back and remember how God made His will known to you, and rejoice that you have the Word of the Lord to sustain you through the challenges in any transition.

It's also normal to mourn what you are leaving behind. Blaine Smith writes:

> No matter how strongly you want a change, you are still leaving behind something cherished. Even the person who is most eager for marriage is forsaking the benefits of single life. It is normal to feel genuine grief over lost benefits. Allow time to work through your feelings, but don't let them hold you back from moving on to God's best.[49]

When you know the will of God you can truly be thankful in every circumstance—having a grateful heart *in* all things, and *for* all things. As we see in the story of Job, the Devil can only do what God allows. So we can trust that our Father will only allow those things into our lives that will promote His ultimate purpose for us—and the God of the Bible is a good God!

---

[49] Smith, Blaine, "Guidance By the Book" © 1992 CBN Publishing, Virginia Beach, VA, P. 145.

In his salutations to the church in Colosse, the apostle Paul mentions his co-laborer:

> Epaphras, who is one of you, a bondservant of Christ, greets you, always laboring fervently for you in prayers, that you may *stand perfect and complete in all the will of God.*
> —Colossians 4:12, NKJV, emphasis added

Paul and Epaphras prayed that the believers would be perfect and complete in the will of God. This verse assures us that we can walk in God's perfect will if we will devote ourselves to hearing God's voice and obeying His commands.

Our Choices and Our Character

Every person is known in two ways:

1. by what we communicate

2. by what we do

You and I are defined by the words we speak and the choices we make. We face decisions in life every day. Some of them are simple and purely natural, such as what to eat for breakfast, which road to take, or what to wear to work. But then there are the life-changing decisions that define who we are and what we will become. These decisions are related to ideas, desires, fantasies, or concepts that can come from either God or Satan. We need to be aware of the fact that we are part of a larger spiritual dimension, in which our decisions play a part. There is a spiritual struggle going on between the Creator of the Universe and Satan. Both God and the Devil want to be expressed through what we say and what we do. In yielding to either of them, your will is involved in the choices you make.

In the process of making a decision on a direction, one's will is employed to choose from the options that are presented to us—both good and evil. The end result of this choice becomes the physical, emotional, and intellectual expressions of who we are as people—and this is how our character is defined. So it is vitally important that we yield our will to God's plan as we seek to make important decisions. Our life is defined by the collection of these choices. Over time, the choices we make will reveal the spiritual direction our lives will take.

Maybe now is the time for you to take an objective look at the direction your life is taking. Paul says if we judge ourselves we will not be judged, but if we do not judge ourselves we will be judged by the Lord... (see 1 Corinthians 11:31-32).

As you read this book you may recognize that your life is in neutral, or it may even be headed in the wrong direction. The good news is that every day is a new beginning in God. Right now you have an opportunity to make a correction in the course of your future. C. S. Lewis said:

> You can't go back and change the beginning, but you can start where you are and change the ending.[50]

Your ability to do this depends upon your obedience to God and His Word. When you look back over your life, how pleased are you with the person your choices have defined?

---

[50] Lewis, C. S. *Essential C. S. Lewis*. Online: www.essentialcslewis.com/confirming-c-s-lewis-quotations-series-overview/

God is giving you an opportunity to make a correction today. If you are willing to see the corrections that need to be made, God will strengthen your will so that you can resist the evil options and choose the good.

It's All About Relationship!

In the quest to hear God's voice and obey His commands, Scripture tells us that:

> If you are willing and obedient, you shall eat the good of the land.
> —Isaiah 1:19, NKJV

Seeking to hear God's voice shows your willingness. Following through in faith and action displays obedience. The Bible promises that if you do these things that God will bless you.

The key is that we seek *Him* and not just what *He can provide*. In the midst of His Sermon on the Mount, Jesus dropped this anchor of truth to keep us balanced:

> Seek the Kingdom of God above all else, and live righteously, and he will give you everything you need.
> —Matthew 6:33, NLT

The point is that we do not seek God for what we can get from Him. We seek Him because we love Him and recognize who He is—the Creator of the universe, the giver of life, the sustainer of all things. He is our Heavenly Father. When we realize His love for us, displayed most dramatically in the sacrifice Jesus made for us at Calvary, we fall in love with

Him, we want to know Him more, and finally, we want to serve Him, hear His voice, and do His will.

The wonderful thing about God is that He rewards us when we do (Hebrews 11:6). He is truly an awesome God!

More than anything, God wants to have a relationship with us as individuals. He's concerned about the things that concern us. He wants to reproduce the attributes of Jesus Christ in our lives. But mostly, He loves us for who we are—and that is a very comforting thought!

Listen to God's plan for us found in Psalm 37:3-5 (comments added by me).

> Trust in the Lord (*have faith in God*); and do good
> > (*good things come from God, so do what He says to do*).
>
> Dwell in the land
> > (*have dominion over everything the Lord brings into your sphere of influence*);
>
> and feed on His faithfulness
> > (*enjoy the peace that comes in knowing that He is true to His word*);
>
> Delight yourself also in the Lord
> > (*fall in love with your Heavenly Father, get to know Him, and do what He tells you to do*);
>
> And He shall give you the desires of your heart
> > (*this is a bonus of seeking first the kingdom of God and His righteousness*);
>
> Commit your way to the Lord
> > (*don't ask God to bless what you're doing, but ask to be doing what He is blessing*);
>
> Trust also in Him
> > (*God is good and can be trusted to give you a future and a hope*);

And He shall bring it to pass
   (every promise of God is conditional, but if we do our part,
   He will most assuredly do His)!
                    —Psalm 37:3-5, NASB, comments mine

If we really want to hear His voice, and if we are truly striving to be obedient to His word, He will plant His thoughts in our heart and our mind. His desires will become our desires. When that happens it is "no sweat" to believe Him for the outcome.

God truly does love you—and He has an amazing plan for your life.

Trusting God's Leading

In His sovereignty, God will lead your life into His kingdom purpose—if you ask Him to do so. God has a grand design for our individual lives and for the world. We can rest in knowing that the Lord truly does order the steps of the righteous person (Psalm 37:23).

When we come to the place of trusting God in His sovereignty, we will also begin to realize that the trials and calamities in life are there to raise a mirror so we can see our real selves. These challenges help to expose sin in our lives that needs to be dealt with—pride, fear, anger, rebellion, insecurity, false humility, negativity, and so on. Just like the pain from a hidden tumor or a ruptured appendix, the difficulties in life, coupled with our reactions to them help us to diagnose sin that needs to be confessed and dealt with. God exposes these things to us so that we will recognize they are there and allow Him to heal and deliver us from them.

The Lord will also often use the difficulties in our lives to woo us back to Himself. When troubles come we need to thank God, and ask Him to do His complete work in the midst of them.

Remember, Satan is God's devil. If God didn't have any use for him, He would have bound him and cast him into the pit after Jesus rose from the dead. But the Lord allows this fallen angel and his demons to operate in this earth because he is the one who creates the needs that drive us to Jesus. God alone rules over all creation. He declared through the prophet Isaiah:

> I am the Lord, and there is no other...
> —Isaiah 45:5, NLT

Nothing takes him by surprise. So Satan only has the power in your life that God allows—and also that you allow.

We are all human. We all make mistakes. God created us and He is well aware of our weaknesses. If you have sinned, repent. If you have made a mistake, learn from it. The biggest mistake in life is wallowing in the sorrow of the past and not learning from the misstep. The only true failure in life is when we fail to get up and start over after we have made the wrong choices.

As you have already learned, this doesn't mean we don't have to diligently seek God on a daily basis. God's sovereignty doesn't negate our responsibility in life. Someone who doesn't rightly balance the truths of God's sovereignty and man's free will might adopt an irresponsible attitude that says, 'whatever is going to happen is going to happen. God already has my life planned out. He'll make sure it all comes together." This is a dangerous position that, sadly, many Christians have adopted.

When God called Billy Graham to a ministry of evangelism at a young age, Billy had to respond to that call and "do" something about it. He had to go to Bible school. He had to formulate a plan for his ministry. He had to start a non-profit corporation. He had to print flyers and take out ads in the media. He had to organize thousands of volunteers. He had to prepare his sermons. He had to get on an airplane and travel to the sight of the rally. And finally he had to preach the Gospel message and give the invitation. When he had done all of those things, God intervened and touched the hearts of the people who heard Billy's message, and they were saved.

We must do our part to walk in the will of God as co-laborers and joint heirs of Jesus Christ. The wonderful plans God has for our life don't just happen—we have to cooperate with the guidance of the Lord by not just "hearing" his voice, but also "doing" His will. But when we step out in faith and do what we believe God is leading us to do, His grace arrives on the scene and amazing things happen—even beyond what we planned.

Our loving Heavenly Father wants to walk with us in the cool of the day as He did with Adam and Eve in the Garden. He wants to bless us so that we can be a blessing to others. And we too can experience the sweet fellowship of knowing God, not only as Lord and Savior, but as a loving Father. God has provided us with these seven keys so that we can learn how to hear His voice and walk in His ways—for His glory and for His Kingdom purposes.

Remember, it's all about relationship.

Questions For Meditation

1. Read Psalm 1:1–3. What will be the end results in the life of someone who's "delight is in the law of the Lord"?

    Oh, the joys of those who do not follow the advice of the wicked, or stand around with sinners, or join in with mockers. But they delight in the law of the Lord, meditating on it day and night. They are like trees planted along the riverbank, bearing fruit each season. Their leaves never wither, and they prosper in all they do.
    —Psalm 1:1-3, NLT

2. What might you be able to do this week to push out the "noise" of the world and focus on hearing God's voice?

3. Explain what this phrase means to you: "receiving guidance from the Lord begins with having a childlike faith."

4. Explain why fasting and prayer is important when making a major decision.

5. How much "peace" do you usually require before moving ahead with a decision? How can you tell the difference between false peace and the peace of the Holy Spirit?

6. In the list of questions to ask yourself when making a decision, which questions stand out to you, and why? If you are facing a major decision right now, which questions are critical to ask at this time?

7. When you look back over your life, how pleased are you with the person your choices have defined?

8. How can the Holy Spirit be a source of power for you in your Christian life and witness?

9. What is it that God has called you to do? Perhaps as you have worked through this book, the Spirit of God has been speaking to your heart. Write down some of the things that you know God has called you to do.

10. Now, write down some ways that you can begin stepping out in faith to "do" what God has called you to.

11. What does the phrase, "it's all about relationship," mean to you?

12. If you wish, write a prayer of dedication and commitment to the Lord to put into practice the things that you have learned—that you would be not just a "hearer" of his word, but a "doer" also.

BIBLIOGRAPHY

Albanes, Rev. Larry. Sermon, First Assembly of God, Erie, PA.

Blackaby, Henry. and Claude King, *Experiencing God* (Nashville: Lifeway, 1993).

Blomgren, David. *Prophetic Gatherings in the Church* (Portland, OR: Bible Temple Publishing, 1979), 59-60.

Bright, Bill. *The Four Spiritual Laws* (Campus Crusade for Christ: 1995).

Burrows, Millar. *What Mean These Stones?* (New York: Meridian, 1956), 52.

Chambers, Oswald. *My Utmost for His Highest.* Online: articles.ochristian.com/article10057.shtml

Dobbins, Richard D. *Seeking God's Will* DayForward online, 2002.

Dobson, James. *Complete Marriage and Family Home Reference Guide* (Carol Stream, IL: Tyndale, 2000).

Fee, Gordon D. and Douglas Stuart. *How to Read the Bible for All Its Worth* (Grand Rapids: Zondervan, 1981), 11.

Fehlauer, Mike. *Exposing Spiritual Abuse* (Lake Mary, FL: Charisma House, 2001).

Finney, Charles G. *Revival Lectures*, "Lecture V: The Prayer of Faith." Amazon Kindle Edition.

Gundry, Robert H. *A Survey of the New Testament* (Grand Rapids: Zondervan, 1994), 87.

Hamon, Bill. *Prophets and Personal Prophecy* (Shippensburg, PA: Destiny Image, 1987), 32.

Harris, R. Laird. *Can I Trust My Bible?* (Chicago: Moody Bible Institute, 1963), 124.

Hayford, Jack, quoted in Cindy Jacobs. *The Voice of God* Ventura, CA: Regal, 1996), 11-12.

Jacobs, Cindy. *The Voice of God*, Ventura, CA: Regal, 1996), 217.

Jeffress, Robert. *Hearing the Master's Voice* (Colorado Springs, CO: Waterbrook, 2001).

Lewis, C. S. *Essential C. S. Lewis*. Online: www.essentialcslewis.com/confirming-c-s-lewis-quotations-series-overview/

Lewis, C. S. *Mere Christianity* (New York: Touchstone, 1943), 144.

Lightner, Robert P. *The Savior and the Scriptures* (Nutley, NJ: Presbyterian and Reformed Publishing, 1970), 28-29.

Mumford, Bob. *Take Another Look at Guidance* (Plainfield, NJ: Logos, 1971), preface.

Osborn, T.L. *The Power of Positive Desire* Tulsa: Harrison House Publishers, 1996.

Pache, Rene. *The Inspiration and Authority of Scripture* (Chicago: Moody Bible Institute, 1969), 124.

Paine, Thomas. *The American Crisis*, December 23, 1776. http://www.ushistory.org/paine/crisis/c-01.htm

Paine, Thomas. *The Crisis*. Good Reads: https://www.goodreads.com/quotes/175410-these-are-the-times-that-try-men-s-souls-the-summer

Robertson, Pat. *12 Principles of God's Guidance* (Virginia Beach, VA: CBN Publishing, 1979).

Robertson, Pat. *Answers to 200 of Life's Most Probing Questions* (Nashville: Thomas Nelson, 1984), 49.

Robertson, Pat, *Bring It On* (Nashville: W. Publishing, 2003), 224-225.

Robertson, Pat with Bob Slosser. *The Secret Kingdom* (Nashville: Thomas Nelson, 1982), 52-54.

Rushnell, Squire D., *When God Winks: How the Power of Coincidence Guides Your Life* (Atria Books, 2002).

Sandford, John and Paula. *The Elijah Task* (Tulsa: Victory House, 1977), 170.

Sherrill, John and Elizabeth. *The Happiest People on Earth* (Grand Rapids: Chosen, 1975), 19-20.

Smith, Blaine. *Guidance by the Book* (Virginia Beach, VA: CBN Publishing, 1992).

Stein, Joseph. *Fiddler on the Roof*, 1971, Metro-Goldwyn-Mayer Studios.

Ten Boom, Corrie. "A Faith Not Hidden," interview by Pat Robertson, *The 700 Club*, Christian Broadcasting Network, 1974.

Tomczak, Larry. *Biblical Confessions to Increase Your Faith*, audio cassette, 1998.

Unger, Merrill F. *The New Unger's Bible Dictionary* (Chicago: Moody Bible Institute, 1988), "plumb line."

Washington, Denzel. Commencement Speech, Dillard University, New Orleans, LA, 2015.

Wesley, John. *Preface to Explanatory Notes upon the Old Testament* (Edinburgh, April 28, 1765).

Westman, Tama. Email to the author.

Williams, Jimmy. *Evidence, Answers, and Christian Faith* (Grand Raids: Kregel, 2002), 95.

Williams, J. Rodman. *Renewal Theology: God, the World, and Redemption* (Grand Rapids: Zondervan, 1988), 37.

Yocum, Bruce. *Prophecy* (Ann Arbor: Servant, 1976), 115.

ABOUT THE AUTHOR

Dr. Craig von Buseck is a published author and Editor of Content for Inspiration.org, the official website of Inspiration Ministries in Charlotte, North Carolina. He is also a contributing writer for CBN.com, ChristianPost.com, *MTL Magazine* mtlmagazine.com, and Generals.org. Craig is a regular guest on Susie Larson's *Live the Promise* program on Faith Radio Network. He holds a Doctor of Ministry and an MA in Religious Journalism from *Regent University*, and a BA in Speech Communication from *Edinboro University of Pennsylvania*.

Craig's books include *Nobody Knows: The Harry T. Burleigh Story* – a narrative biography of the great African-American composer who led the way in making the African-

American Spirituals known to the world. Craig is also the author of *Praying the News: Your Prayers Are More Powerful than You Know*, co-written by 700 Club co-host Wendy Griffith.

Craig's new biography about President Truman and the Zionist Movement, *I Am Cyrus: Harry S. Truman and the Rebirth of Israel*, will be published in spring of 2019 by Lighthouse Publishers of the Carolinas.

Craig has extensive speaking experience and travels often to conferences, professional events, churches, and writer training meetings. Craig served for twelve years as Ministries Director and Programming Director for CBN.com, one of the world's most popular Christian websites. He also served for more than ten years on the Executive Board of the Internet Evangelism Coalition (IEC).

Learn more at **vonbuseck.com**

facebook.com/craigvonbuseck
twitter.com/craigvonbuseck
linkedin.com/in/craigvonbuseck/
cbn.com/about/bios/craigvonbuseck.aspx

www.ingramcontent.com/pod-product-compliance
Lightning Source LLC
Chambersburg PA
CBHW071152070526
44584CB00019B/2763